Black Hat
Banking

Also By M. Blaine Faulkner

- Invisible Banking: An introduction to Offshore Banking and Asset Protection

BLACK HAT BANKING

A Hacker's Guide to Financial Security & Privacy

BOOK **1** Covert Core

M. BLAINE FAULKNER

To those that wish to make "Following the Money" an impossible task.

Table of Contents

"Those who would sacrifice essential liberty to purchase a little temporary safety, deserve neither liberty or safety."

Benjamin Franklin

Introduction

To call oneself a "black hat" hacker is tantamount to admitting to being a criminal. Considering the title of this book, one has to ask why somebody would do such a thing. Logically one might assume I was some minor league hacker that has spent a year in a US minimum Security Federal Prison Camp already, and now I am writing about my awesome experiences in cybercrime. One could be forgiven for assuming that I might have been rehabilitated by the correctional system, seen the light, and now I'm on a path to help humanity.

Actually, I don't know that we could forgive anyone for thinking something that ludicrous. A trip to prison in the US is more likely to lead to gang membership, drug use, and/or death than rehabilitation or book publishing, but I digress. An important first step for this adventure in enlightenment will be understanding where this illicit information comes from. Thus I have to tell you a little bit about who I am, and what I did. So before we go any further down the rabbit hole, please allow me to introduce myself.

Hello, I'm CygonX, and I'm a hacker. But unfortunately the term "hacker" paints the picture with too broad of a brush. Having said I'm a hacker, it's impossible to know if I mean I'm a "White Hat" hacker, working for the good of humanity, or a "Black Hat" hacker, stealing financial data for profit. The term is even mistakenly used to describe "script kiddies". These would-be criminals lack any skill whatsoever but usually buy or lease crimeware to steal data. But we can quibble about the exact terminology later. For the moment, I can say with complete certainty that I meet all the criteria for the popular definition of the term "hacker" per the United States Attorney's Office, the Federal Bureau of Investigations, and the US News Media.

It's been said that I have defaced websites, conducted massive spam operations, poisoned DNS servers, and conducted Distributed Denial of Service attacks. Some have said that I've ran clusters of automated exploit scanners, and that I have been involved in a variety of high level penetrations. The FBI once referred to my software security blog as the Internet's oldest Mecca for software piracy. It's a matter of court record that my network security blog, Black Security Group, once got me sued for allegedly outing an ISP that deployed all their customers routers with default passwords.

The result was the complete collapse of Internet service for an entire city.

With substantial input from law enforcement, the media cast me in the most nefarious role possible. As if I wasn't hated quite enough as a "super hacker" I was unceremoniously bestowed the title of real life "super villain". It's been reported that I was deeply involved in the arms trade, and that at any given time I could be found armed with a matched pair of exotic handguns. One Texas reporter has even repeatedly inferred that I have gotten away with murder, while each new report seems to find a way to work in machine guns and explosives. An Assistant US Attorney (that's a federal prosecutor) tied it all together when she told the press that although I was clearly a genius, I was a "truly evil" one. Which would seemingly be a job requirement for their more recent conclusion, which is that I'm the de facto Chief of Technology for a certain Mexican cartel.

By this point you might be thinking that if any of the above is true, then I'm a horrible person, and I should be locked up post haste. If so, you are in luck. After a series of FBI raids in 2009 I began my life as an international fugitive, eventually landing me a Red Warrant with Interpol. In 2010, an FBI rendition team kidnapped my family and me from Cancun. I was returned to the US, and later sentenced to 30 years in federal prison. However, it wasn't my hacking exploits that got me arrested, it was my other life.

Hello, my name is Michael Blaine Faulkner, former Chief Executive Officer of Crydon Capital Corporation. This private equity company was established as a vehicle to manage merger and acquisition activities in the tech sector. Together with several other partners, we launched VoIP (Voice over Internet Protocol) companies, Internet Service Providers (ISP), Hosting Companies, international telecommunications ventures, and credit card processing platforms.

With my extensive background in database engineering, IT infrastructure, telecommunications, and e-commerce applications, I was the perfect fit for this type of new technology investment and development. As a hands-on CEO, I oversaw every stage of corporate development, and eked out record profits in highly competitive industries. We took on entrenched service providers and waged corporate warfare with the mighty sword of open-source platforms. Our aggressive growth model forced down prices in the industry, increased reliability, and brought new services to end-users. The Crydon family of companies was a force to be reckoned with in the tech sector, right up until we bumped heads with the NSA's illegal surveillance platform.

The Crydon company Intellivox specialized in Wholesale VoIP. We cornered the market on routes into Mexico by engineering our own direct connections. Using free-space-optics and microwave repeaters, we jumped the border with no need to rent routes across AT&T's network, the way it was usually done. In fact, we also skipped direct access to Mexico's largest telecom company, Telmex. We used GSM channel-bank technology. For the non-technical, this means we piped calls from the US directly into Mexico's cellular networks via a VoIP tunnel. From our perspective, we helped hundreds of companies offer discounted calling card programs to end users, while providing high quality service. As an afterthought, we even encrypted the route between the countries to protect our customer's privacy for the through-the-air length of the route.

What we didn't know at the time is that we had effectively taken over 60% of all the telecommunications traffic to Mexico. As the country spans the United States' entire southern border, this was apparently of some strategic concern to the US government. As this traffic was kept within our private network, none of the NSA's back-door deals with AT&T and Verizon allowed the US Government access to the unencrypted call streams. We had inadvertently blinded the US surveillance systems, and interrupted dozens of active investigations. Granted, most of these cases were the DEA's for-profit seizure operations, but the US Government was quite upset all the same.

Although I later joked that the FBI could have just called up and said "pretty please" for live-stream access to that data, that's just not how they operate. Since I was an outspoken Libertarian and "cryptoanarchist", I was already an enemy to their big government agenda. In March of 2009 the FBI sent a heavily armed 40 man Entry Team into my home in Southlake, Texas. After terrifying my wife and three young children, they seized everything electronic: Playstations, Xboxes, Cable Box DVRs, Phones, and all the computers. They also hit a Crydon Technology data-center in Dallas. Hundreds of servers were taken off-line, very few of which had anything to do with the Intellivox VoIP operations. Thousands of hosting and VoIP customers lost their service.

So began the FBI case that would last 3 years, and cost the US Government over $65 million dollars. They meticulously filtered 200 terabytes of data to concoct a fraud case to dump on 22 tech executives, managers, and accounting personnel. Sensing subterfuge, and with no real belief in the possibility of a fair trial, I left the US.

I started a new life for my family in Mexico, and continued that life right up until we were kidnapped by the FBI. In spite of the fact that the case involved no drugs, no guns, no violence, and no actual human "victims", over 120 years of prison time was handed down in this case. In a country where the average sentence for murder is under 23 years, we were given 30 and 40 year sentences for accidentally interfering with US surveillance operations, all under the guise of committing fraud against the multi-billion dollar behemoths of AT&T and Verizon.

Please note, AT&T has a quarterly loss reserve of $900 million. That's to say, that they expect to lose $3.6 billion a year to fraud, abuse, and bad debt. In no way, shape, or form did the $6 million in corporate debt between our companies affect their bottom line.

For years I struggled to understand how the government could destroy so many lives for the alleged non-payment of bills between telecom companies. It didn't make sense. In spite of my past exploits, or even the things I did while I was "on the run", the way the government demonized us in the media was beyond strange. In a country that has serial killers, pedophiles, and mass murderers, they were referring to a rogue telecom executive as "truly evil". The evidence in this case was simply mountains of emails taken out of context to misconstrue corporate debt and aggressive business practices as overt fraud.

None of the 30 plus defense attorneys in this case had ever seen anything like it. From prison, I worked meticulously for almost two years to prepare my defense. We prepared a perfect HTML multi-media presentation, complete with links to exhibits and explanations. I planned to go to trial from the very beginning, and I planned to win. However, days before we were to pick a jury, I was made an offer.

At the time of the US Attorney's offer my wife and I had already spent over two years in custody. My wife was in bad health, and US Marshal Services had denied the expense of medical testing requested by the facility where she was housed. As my wife had nothing to do with any of my businesses, we had known all along she was being held as leverage against me. After her third trip to the emergency room, I would have done anything to get her out of jail, and the prosecution was well aware of that fact. I was told that if I agreed to sign a plea my wife would be released on bail immediately to get the medical testing she needed, and that she'd be guaranteed to receive no more than 5 years in prison once sentenced. That same plea would guarantee me a 20 year sentence, but my lawyers assured me it wouldn't be much more than that.

Under that severe level of duress, I signed the plea. Four other defendants went to trial, two were acquitted, and everyone else took a plea for 10 years or less. Of the two that lost at trial, one received a 9 year sentence. The other, then 25 years old with no criminal history, received a 40 year prison sentence. In spite of my lawyer's assurances, I received the 30 year maximum they could give me under the plea. Again, we were lead to believe, as was the jury, that all of this was due to the fact that our companies didn't pay AT&T and Verizon for telecom services.

This case had more "electronic discovery" than all other cases before it; over twice the data used in the Enron case. The defense was buried in this discovery, yet all the data the defense requested was unavailable. In response to the volume of evidence in the case, Forbes magazine reported that our case had become Kafkaesque. The Electronic Frontier Foundation immediately objected to the obvious "general" warrant, and over-broad search and seizure. Many of our clients sued the FBI for the government's seizure of servers critical to their business operations. Wired magazine did a very balanced story on the early stages of the case, but eventually the national media coverage faded. The case was all but forgotten everywhere but Reddit, where netizens hashed out the details of the case for a bit longer. Then the formerly high profile case was shoved into the annals of the internet, and the defendants were shipped off to prison. Their appeals are of course ongoing.

I'm sure many of you would find the details of my adventures quite interesting. I have often thought of writing a book on the whole story. I'd have to cover the adventure that spanned across US, Mexico, Panama, and Honduras, where I am alleged to have faked my own death. I'd also have to include the scene where we were chased through the back alleys of Monterrey Mexico by the Federal

Police. I'd even have to explain how Hillary Clinton's visit to Mexico almost got us killed. And I am sure many readers would love to hear how a merry band of international fugitives hacked the FBI, the telecoms, the banks, and multiple corporations, all in the doomed attempt to prove their innocence. But that's not what this is about.

My apologies for the diversion, but I felt it necessary to explain the context of my crusade before delving into the world of big data and financial surveillance systems. You see, ever since this debacle began I've struggled to make sense of it. Eventually I figured out why we were targeted, and ironically in some ways I have to agree with the conclusions the government came to.

So here I am, with my life completely destroyed for something I didn't do, but I've had to admit that I may have come to the same conclusions if I was working with the same data.

That's the real problem, big data doesn't display the full worth of a human life, as it can only return the exact data that has been queried. After hundreds of Freedom of Information Act filings, and thousands of hours spent combing through terabytes of electronic discovery, patterns began to emerge. Comparing these patterns to other federal case law has led me to some very dark and ominous conclusions.

With these patterns in mind, I sought out the people that would know exactly how big data systems are abused. In most cases, criminals aren't generally very forthcoming with the secret sauce of their revenue streams, but my infamous reputation opened a lot of doors for me that would be closed to most journalist. I was able to interview dozens of cybercriminals, cartel members, lawyers, pedophiles, bank executives, bank robbers, and law enforcement officers.

With all due respect to traditional journalistic technique, you can't really get to know someone until you have been locked in a box with them for a few weeks at a time. And it's hard to get the truth out of someone when they are still concerned about their careers, but nothing alleviates those concerns like a lengthy prison sentence.

With a complete understanding of the underlying technology, I knew just the right questions to ask. Slowly, all the pieces came together, and with them, the understanding of how and why big data is used and abused. Armed with these intimate details of criminal techniques, corporate profiteering, and sweeping government overreach, I empowered my unincarcerated associates to assist me.

Together we've compiled such a volume of research material that no one with any kind of life whatsoever would ever have time to review and process it. Fortunately for my readers, the US Government has given me plenty of time to work on this project, as they took my life from me long ago. Here in the Covert Core Series, we have compiled comprehensive proof of exactly how these systems are utilized by governments, criminals, and corporations.

From experience, I can say that there is nothing more boring than reading technical specifications, white-papers, RFCs, or case law. I believe the aforementioned groups depend on that fact. And so it is with great honor that I bring these dirty facts to light for all to read in plain English with real-life examples of exactly how these systems penetrate our lives in the most sinister of ways, and what you can do to prevent it.

Preface

Having read the introduction to this book one could understandably have some concerns about the author's moral and ethical positions. First and foremost, I'm no saint, nor do I pretend to be. I have done some very bad things, and I will likely do so again. It's unfortunate that I've been forced to live this kind of life, but it's the life that has made collecting this information possible. That being said, the only alleged "victims" of my alleged "crimes" are multi-billion dollar corporations. If that makes a difference to some people, so be it. If anyone cares to read more on the federal case, more information can be found on my website. Personally, I don't believe the US will ever let me out of prison, and I have resigned myself to that fate. That's just the way it is. What should matter to all involved is not how this information came to light as much as what this information means, and how it affects you.

In this book we have to address specific types of systems used by the government, corporations, and hackers. It is not my intention to infer that only the US Government uses these systems, as that's certainly not the case. But as the United States has poured the most time and money into surveillance systems, they make the perfect case study for a "worst case scenario" discussion.

Additionally, it is not my intention to criticize the programmers for these systems. I'm not one to blame gun manufacturers for mass shootings, and I certainly can't blame technology companies for what governments and criminals do with their software. For that reason, I will avoid mentioning specific software packages where possible. It should also be noted that these companies change their product names as soon as there is the least little bit of negative publicity, and most don't seem to be married to their company name either. What's important is what the software does, and who's using it, not the name of the package or the vendor's name. That's especially true since cybercriminals often use custom versions based on open-source software, which would have no name at all.

Regarding the actual intelligence agencies, there will be those that view this book as an act of treason, or worse. It's become apparent that there are die hard patriots that believe the US can do no wrong, and that the US Government should be trusted with ultimate power to run the planet. I assume these people never travel outside the US, or have any idea how the rest of the world views the United States. Maybe they even tune out the inconvenient statistics associated with US drone strikes, or US foreign policy in general. These people probably even believe that the whole world wants and needs American style democracy. Although these topics are fascinating in their own right, it is not my intent to promote or criticize any particular political ideology, crazy as some may be. Though in the discussion of personal privacy we'll have to take a bit of a Libertarian position by definition.

The point of this work is to explore this technology, not to ruffle the feathers of the true believers, or to push a political agenda. If this book becomes an issue for any US intelligence agency, I'm sure they have assassins on speed-dial, so we'll all find out soon enough.

Regardless of my personal problems with the US government, it's not my intention to dilute the effectiveness of US intelligence or Law Enforcement operations by disclosing this material. I do not now, nor have I ever, supported terrorism. I do however recognize how this information could benefit a terrorist organization, in theory. In reality, any organization with the resources to attack the US would seemingly also have the resources to do their homework on US surveillance systems themselves. Furthermore, I did not have to utilize my background in advanced mathematics to calculate the odds of any one US citizen being harmed in a terrorist attack.

According to analysis done by Human Rights Watch, the number of mass shootings in the US for 2015 was 355. The number perpetrated by Muslims was only 3. The chances of an American being killed in a terror attack by someone claiming that their actions were justified by Islam are 1 in 20,000,000. As compared to the odds of a US citizen being killed by a dog which is 1 in 116,448. And so we have to ask, why isn't there a "War on Dogs"? The answer to that is simple, you don't need million dollar missiles to kill dogs. If such Super Dogs do emerge, I' m quite sure the military defense contractors will step up to the plate and lobbyists will carry briefcases full of dog killing money to congress. That's how the military industrial complex works in a country that has been engaged in perpetual warfare since its inception.

US citizens should be outraged by the targeted assassinations in the Middle-East, and the civilian casualties of the US drone programs. That would be the humane response, but understandably

18

no one wants to think about that, much less put their lives on the line to question it. Investigative journalists like Glen Greenwald and Jeremy Scahil seem to be the brave exceptions. However, if Super Dogs began tearing apart school buses in the suburbs, then Americans would surely stand up. It's always a wake-up call when it begins happening in your own backyard. That's when it's time to act, right?

Well folks, the US military industrial complex is spinning up products and services aimed squarely at the US domestic surveillance market. That's right, Raytheon, Northrop-Grumman, Lockheed-Martin, and virtually every company that's ever made a dime from government weapons systems are now developing "cyberwarfare systems". These systems all utilize big data. In the massive collections of geolocational data, if you run just the right query, you can even find your own backyard.

With all due respect to the big government contractors, terrorists would have to begin killing many thousands of US citizens before the math would make sense. In my opinion, the value of Civil Liberties and true personal freedom far exceeds any protection US intelligence agencies can claim to provide via all-inclusive domestic surveillance. Maybe I'm the true believer, but I'd gladly give my own life to protect the privacy and freedom of the entire population. So I have to disagree with the US government's constant assertion that they need more power to prevent "terrorism". The correct solution to prevent terrorism is, and will always be, to adjust US foreign policy.

My position is that human beings should not be treated like the data that represents them. When a single person dies a violent death, it's often a crime. When dozens die, it's referred to as a tragedy. When thousands die, those are just statistics. Well, except when it happens in the US, as it did on 9/11. Thus, it is concerning that big data is making it much easier for those in power to view smaller and smaller groups of people as merely statistics. Meanwhile, the position of those in power continues to be that they need more power to provide better security for everyone. Oversight, transparency, and limited government be damned, they just need more power. Until such a point that the targeting and tracking algorithms are made available for public scrutiny and democratic proceedings, no government should be allowed to arbitrarily conduct mass surveillance. That being said, I certainly understand it would be Utopian, if not outright science-fiction, to envision a future where the citizens vote on lines of code. Meanwhile, as the no-fly list isn't published, I'm quite certain no other government database will be either.

Ironically, the same groups of people that think the US should have unfettered access to all data, also think the US should lead the free world. Perhaps they haven't yet processed the fact that other countries might actually follow the lead of the US in tracking their own citizens, as Syria has. Hundreds of anti-government sympathizers have been tracked down and abducted already, and barrel bombs tend to fall on areas where specific cell phones gather. The Syrian government might say that their targeting algorithm is: "Target only if "enemies" (dissidents) is greater than 5, and civilians is 0". But based on the extensive civilian casualties, I think we can agree that is not the algorithm they are using. So let us next ask what the algorithm is for a US drone strike. Maybe it's "High Value Targets greater than 1, and civilians 0". But again, we know that's not the algorithm based on the sheer number of civilian casualties. More importantly, who voted on the algorithm they are using, and who voted on the ones used for the US domestic surveillance operations now?

Since we all know there will be no vote on algorithms any time soon, we have to pursue a different path.

Forward

Books like this are not written in a vacuum, in spite of my current environment. This project stands on the shoulders of many journalists, and other authors as well. More than any others, I owe a debt to Edward Snowden for his heroic acts, and to Glen Greenwald for his detailed account of the Snowden saga in his book "No Place to Hide". Before Snowden's revelations we were juggling conspiracy theories trying to figure out why the Department of Justice (DOJ) would spend $65 million dollars to thoroughly hammer citizens for unpaid phone bills. Granted, some of us in telecom had known AT&T was in bed with the NSA since even before 2005 when whistle-blower Mark Klein disclosed the details of the AT&T/NSA nexus. Those of us that have spent thousands of hours in multi-carrier meet-me-rooms (where telecommunication providers interconnect their networks), have seen the now infamous red door to nowhere. But like most Americans, I wasn't bothered by the police state until it knocked on my door. Before Snowden, all those conspiracy theories just seemed far-fetched.

Having read the works of Greenwald and many others, I wanted to present this new information as professionally and as unbiased as they had. It was my intention to be non-biased, nonpolitical, and to report the facts without my personal insights or opinions. In the original rough drafts of this book, I actually did a pretty good job of that. But there was a problem. People didn't get it. Even for those that had previously read "No Place to Hide", and other detailed accounts of the emerging global police state, it just didn't compute for the average citizen. The technology is just too abstract.

Case in point, if I was to quote directly from my Freedom of Information Act sources, even the more technical of my readers might not get it. For example, if I was to say "based on the reconciliation of cellular carrier data preservation policies with the Department of Justice's stated purpose of the program, long term records can be parsed at a later date in relationship to current files across multiple end-user accounts." That sounds innocent enough, right? Even if you factor in the fine print that the data includes geolocational data it still doesn't click for most people. If I was a true journalist, maybe I would leave it at that, and let the readers do the math themselves. If I was scared of my government, or had anything left to lose, that's probably exactly what I'd do. My family and friends would no doubt agree that would be the safer path. But how would that move the needle between oppression and freedom? Let us throw caution to the wind and look at that line again, in plain English.

Your cellular carrier will store all the data it can technically gather for as long as it possibly can, and the government will have access to that data into perpetuity. But we've known that since Snowden's leaks, it's just "metadata", right? Your metadata includes Cell Site Location Information (CSLI) and geolocational data. We'll discuss the difference between those two shortly, but what's important here is that with that data any government official, giant corporation, or criminal organization can easily resolve the details of your life: your associates, your daily travel routines, your significant other's identity, who your children are, what doctor's you visit, your favorite restaurant, your place of business, and a long list of other detailed analytics.

This data can yield exactly the amount of time you spend in what bar, or what church, and who you are there with. If your phone has ever gone to a hotel with another phone that doesn't belong to your spouse, that's in a database somewhere. With a single database search any of the aforementioned groups can generate a comprehensive report on you, and use further data points to build a complete picture of you as a person, at least as seen by machines through an algorithm. Those are the facts, and that's how big data works.

With that in mind, I have opted to write the Covert Core Series for actual human beings in a way that real people can digest and process, without needing a degree in Computer Science.

In response to examples in this book, like the one above, many groups will say "Oh, but we'd never do that." Maybe AT&T and Verizon don't actually track their customers based on marital fidelity, but that's of little consequence since they sell their data. "But at least the government oversees that data, right?" Not so much. The biggest data vendors are actually governments themselves. At the root of modern society, all data is for sale, and it will be used by anyone that can make a dime off it. If you are so inclined to believe in the best of humanity, I wish you the best in all your future endeavors, but you should probably put this book down now.

With all due respect to the authors and journalists that have come before me, I respect their safe and non-biased reporting. Had

I compiled my data from public sources and from interviewing government insiders and corporate executives, I'm sure I would have come up with a more optimistic conclusion as well. However, as the bulk of my material originates from Federal Case Law, Freedom of Information Act filings, and interviews with dirty cops, cartel members, pedophiles, and cybercriminals, I have arrived at a darker place.

For example, if you read the policy of the State of Florida regarding the sale of their driver's license data, it clearly says they do their utmost to vet the companies they sell the data to. We all want to believe that the $62 million the State of Florida makes per year selling that data is only to those vetted companies. However, when sitting in a prison cell with a cybercriminal that explains how easy it is to get that data, I have to question that vetting process. Reading court documents from that cybercriminal's federal case, I was left with little doubt that the only vetting the State of Florida does is verifying that they receive payment for the data.

In spite of really wanting to believe the best of humanity myself, and to trust the governments of the world, I just can't do that anymore.

Regardless if you paid for a signed hard-copy of this book, or stole an ebook copy via a Torrent site, I owe it to you the reader to convey the most accurate information possible. I will do so while sparing you the lies and platitudes of those in power. And so we must briefly suspend our natural desire to think the best of our fellow man, and pursue the more statistically likely possibilities. If a government can use the data to accumulate power, they will. If a corporation can turn a profit with the data, they will do so. If a criminal organization can make a dollar, that's what they'll do. With those ugly truths in mind, I've been able to fill in a lot of blanks, and to dig down to the core of the big data problem.

Author's Note

The Covert Core Series explores what is, for many, very delicate and controversial subjects. My primary goal was to illuminate technology that is frequently discussed, but rarely thoroughly examined. Along the way I tried to set my personal views aside and to be as objective as possible. Admittedly, my own global libertarian viewpoint does come through. I've found it impossible to write about the use of this technology by large organizations without mentioning its obvious effect on the personal freedoms of individuals. Many readers will question my intent behind writing about this subject at all, and express concern at the information revealed in this book. Although my intention was never to provide a guide to criminal or immoral activity, this book does contain material that some will find objectionable.

As a devout advocate for privacy, I felt obligated to protect the privacy of the people that were interviewed for this book, especially in instances where the subject didn't realize they were being interviewed. Where necessary, I have altered personal names, screen names, and identity information. In several instances I found it advantageous to merge several individuals into a single composite character as well. I have tried to balance individual rights with the social benefits that come from describing these people and their world. Any errors or omissions are mine alone. I apologize in advance for any inconvenience or distress caused to anyone featured in this book.

This technology is evolving. By the time you finish reading Black Hat Banking, much of this technology will have changed its face, and added features. New laws will be written, and global policies will shift, but at its core big data problems will unfortunately remain the same.

Apologies

Law enforcement will be quick to point out the fact that this book explains exactly how some of their systems work, which could benefit cybercriminals. By that same token, cybercriminals will no doubt be upset with me for pointing out how they are already abusing these same technologies. Although I am cognizant of the fact that many of my readers are law enforcement, and cybercriminals, I didn't write this book to benefit either group. This book was written for the citizens caught in the middle of the conflict escalation on all sides. But I suppose I should apologize in advance all the same.

Concerning Law Enforcement, if your agency hasn't ever lied to a grand jury, fabricated evidence, coerced a witness, or misconstrued technical data to benefit the prosecution, then please accept my apologies. If your department has never trampled civil rights, targeted the innocent, or ran for-profit seizure operations, then it's certainly not my intention to make your job more difficult. I respect the work done to serve and protect citizens, especially when you can do that job without shooting unarmed minorities, the mentally ill, or innocent bystanders. Obviously I must be referring to some other country's law enforcement than that of the United States of America, because the US is now the land of mass incarceration with unchecked abuse of conspiracy laws, and forced plea agreements.

However, if you represent law enforcement in any of the 192 other countries with a lower per-capita prison population, then please do accept my apologies if my disclosures make your job more difficult.

Concerning lesser cybercriminals, if you haven't destroyed anyone's life by stealing their identity, then I hope this book doesn't get you arrested. If you haven't ruined personal credit it took decades for a law abiding citizen to build, then I am truly sorry if this book complicates your life. If you haven't held a hospital's computer network hostage with ransom-ware, then I do apologize for outing your techniques, tactics, and technologies. However, if you are so inclined to victimize individuals, then I do hope to see you soon, here with me, in Federal Prison.

Concerning the large corporations, I am sure you have the resources to adapt to anything I disclose here. You will lose your ability to track the more savvy readers that can make use of this information, but I am sure you will find a method to make up for that in a way that is pleasing to your investors. If not, you can sue me. Just get in line behind Uncle Sam, whom I already owe $18,242,752.47 for the arbitrary extrapolation of commercial debt between telecom companies.

Concerning the professional criminal organizations that only target large banks, large corporations, and governments; I am truly sorry if any of the material in this book makes your job any more difficult. Really.

And to you the reader, I apologize for having to drag you through all the ugly details of how this information came to light. It is my hope that with the newly informed perspective this information can be better understood in the context in which it was discovered.

The Covert Core Series

We are at a precipice. The bulk of human knowledge thus far is now available to anyone with internet access. With equal ease and convenience anyone in the first world can access stock prices, weather reports, the formula for gun powder, or a list of exploits for the latest version of the Windows Operating System. Although most people waste this great resource on mindless entertainment, there are select groups of people that have figured out the means to utilize this access for illicit purposes and often immense personal gain. Along with those in it for the money are the spooks operating on behalf of governments, and a fair number of freedom fighters working against many oppressive government agendas. Whatever your agenda is, this data access has become a great equalizer for all humanity.

For the first time in human history everyone truly has the potential to make great change in the world, regardless of national borders, class, or personal circumstances. Unfortunately this technology hasn't been purely positive for mankind. We are all still human. Politicians sell the souls of their constituents to garner favor with military defense contractors. Scam artists steal senior citizen's medical data and pilfer millions from insurance companies. Transnational criminal organizations using armies of hackers seize computers of hospitals and schools, holding them for ransom. It's open warfare, and to rely on your government to defend you is a foolhardy idea at best. Hackers often use repurposed tools stolen from government agencies for some of their largest hacks.

If the US government can't protect the National Security Agency's secret tool box, they certainly can't protect your business or your bank account. We've simply past the point where we can pretend like it's all going to work out. Now it's time to learn the techniques to play the game yourself, or accept the fact that you are merely a number in a database, fully at the mercy of the government and hackers alike.

The intent of The Covert Core Series is to give would-be operators a road map for the effective utilization of modern technology to play the game on equal footing with the intelligence agencies, hackers, and criminals that are shaping the lives of the less informed.

Covert Core is about taking your life back from the databases that track you, and opting out of mass surveillance. It's about arming regular people with these techniques for your own agenda, whatever that may be, instead of allowing yourself to be used by others wielding the power of big data. All the tools and tricks of black hat hackers, white collar criminals, federal agents, and government spies are available to every single human on Earth. Due to years of informational warfare between all of the above, everything imaginable has been leaked to the internet. Today an operator can learn how to hack a power plant, how to build a firewall, or now the proper techniques for offshore banking and asset protection. All the information is available somewhere.

Here, the ultimate goal of The Covert Core Series is individual empowerment and freedom; the libertarian idea that we each should choose our own path in life, free of outside manipulation. Information is power, and the most informed win. These books were written in celebration of information that wants to be free. What you do with it is entirely up to you.

About Invisible Banking

Since my book "Invisible Banking" was published in 2011 the financial climate has changed considerably. Passed in late 2010, the American Foreign Compliance Tax Act (FACTA) has forced more US Citizens abroad to dump their US citizenship to protect their wealth. BitCoin has matured, evolved, and grown into a valuable tool in the process of wealth protection. Panama has become fully compliant with US demands, and ceased to be a secure Offshore Financial Center (OFC) for US citizens. Liberty Reserve, once a leading virtual currency has since been shut down by US law enforcement, and all of their accounts seized by the government. US law enforcement agencies continue to ramp up their seizure operations to shore up their reduced operations budgets. None of the above is good news for anyone that believes they should be allowed to keep their wealth unencumbered by erratic government policy driven by poor fiscal responsibility.

In spite of the current heavy handed tactics deployed by debt ridden first world nations, there is some silver lining. Now, more than ever before, there are reliable virtual currencies in play running on secure servers outside of hostile jurisdictions. Additionally, as bad government continues to swell the ranks of the poor, new solutions for the "unbanked" have emerged, that can be repurposed for asset protection. The new threats to wealth have forced a whole new level of creativity in the underground economies. Today the deep web exceeds the size of the surface internet, and for good reason, but there is no official bank for the dark web just yet.

As the police state clamps down on civil liberties more people find it advantageous to become expatriates of their birth country. It's never been easier to telework, learn a new language, or travel incognito. All of the tools to be a free and happy global citizen are now available.

Our original plan was to simply publish a second edition to Invisible Banking, and to toe the line of political correctness, avoiding the discussion of anything legally sensitive in the US. The problem is that we can't have an honest discussion about what is and isn't possible if we have to continuously refine the bounds of our discussion to what's not frowned upon in the super power police states. This is especially problematic when the powers that be are constantly devising new ways to monitor and control commerce and personal wealth. Since 2011 we have received a large number of emails from a diverse group of people asking for expansion of the topics covered in Invisible Banking. Unfortunately the answers to today's problems with financial privacy can no longer be solved with merely offshore banking and asset protection schemes.

In the US there are now scores of entrepreneurs involved in the legal (at the state level) marijuana industry that have few banking options. With the growing popularity of "gray area" products and services on the dark web financial surveillance systems pose a very real problem for freedom loving people worldwide. Many of us believe that what someone chooses to do in the privacy of their own home, that doesn't affect the rights of others, need not be regulated by a government. In spite of the growing number of libertarians that oppose big government inventions such as mass incarceration and Draconian prison sentences, first world governments continue to pass thousands of pages of new laws each year. The US alone has 20,000 pages of criminal law that defines the finite limits of "freedom".

Meanwhile, oblivious American citizens continue to trade their civil liberties for "security" while enriching the cyber-industrial complex, with no net gain in personal security.

Fortunately, it's still 100% possible to avoid monitoring by the police state's financial surveillance apparatus, but offshore banking alone is no longer the answer. Black Hat Banking is a collection of topics describing the tools you'll need to conduct business, maintain personal wealth, and achieve a higher level of freedom, without getting vectored by a nation state and targeted for investigation. Have no doubts, law enforcement agencies do indeed augment their budgets with seizures, and they do so without a hearing or formal finding of guilt. It happens every day, and the total take is in the billions. With that in mind, this book had to include many more techniques for asset protection, with much more background than the original Invisible Banking.

Additionally, the threat of a technologically evolved level of transnational crime makes new headlines every day. When a government or large retail outlet is targeted, it makes the news.

When they hit you personally or your business, you can bet it won't be on CNN. And for that reason in Black Hat Banking we've had to address the very real threat of organized efforts in the areas of financial crime. It's unfortunate that all the tax dollars spent to

32

arm the cyber-industrial complex don't trickle down to protect small businesses, and entrepreneurs, but governments aren't exactly known for efficient use of tax dollars. And thus it is up to each of us to protect ourselves first, and here we discuss the best ways to do that.

However, for the many fans of the original Invisible Banking, all the material covered in the original publication of Invisible Banking has been fully updated and included here in Black Hat Banking. Enjoy.

Chapter 1: Anti-American?

Throughout this book we'll discuss the manifestation of financial surveillance systems in which it is often necessary to mention the United States of America as they have the largest infrastructure in place for this type of surveillance.

In the past few years I have been accused of having views contrary to that of the general "American" narrative. Members of the Department of Justice have even called me anti-American. Somewhat ironically, they did kidnap me and bring me back to the United States to tell me that. It seems that if you don't fully support their agenda then you are the enemy, and thus subject to the full might of the empire. However, I feel I need to comment on the notion of one being anti-American, or anti-government. As these two labels represent very different things, I will address them separately.

Concerning the citizens of the United States of America, I do truly wish them all the best in all their many endeavors. I hold no ill will towards the citizenry for what their government has done to me or the world at large. However, I do believe Americans spend way too much time focused on leisure activities such as reality television and sports, versus potentially more productive activities in education or global politics. In fact, I think Americans are largely checked-out on world affairs, and blissfully unaware of America's current place in the world. Any economist with at least a B in math can look at the national debt and tell you that there is eventually going to be a reckoning. Yet your average American can't name a single Senator or Congressman for their state.

Meanwhile, the US Government runs around the planet enforcing their world-view on other nations and creating new terrorists with each misguided assault on other countries, cultures, and religions. Which would be tolerable if it truly was the cost of doing business on the path to world peace, but it's not. It's just more war to support the profit margins of the military industrial complex that support the politicians in Washington. US Citizens could be at fault for what their government has become, but that is truly none of my concern.

There are bumper stickers that say, "America, if you don't like it, leave." That's a good point. There are 193 countries to choose from, and no reason to believe you necessarily would be born into the one that will suit you best for your entire life. People have migrated for hundreds of years for a variety of reasons. With politics, climate change, globalization, varying laws, and access to technology, there are just more reasons to move. For me personally, I simply prefer countries that are less insular, and less of a nanny state. I agree with the late great George Carlin, the world needs less warning labels. And if I had to pick a country, maybe I'd pick one that hadn't spent billions of taxpayer dollars to build illegal surveillance platforms to monitor its own citizens. So I don't hate America, I just have a myriad of reasons as to why I prefer to live elsewhere. I personally believe if Americans had traveled half as much as I have, many would prefer to live elsewhere as well.

Concerning the US Government, I don't hate them either. Sure, I'm in Federal Prison with a 30-year sentence for something I didn't do, and I'm not happy about that. But neither the senate nor the house voted to have me indicted. I got wrapped up in a broad and sweeping abuse of power under the guise of national security concerns. Even though I watched FBI agents and US Attorneys lie repeatedly and fabricate evidence, they did that because they truly believed I was the enemy. In their own eyes, they are heroes.

Now somewhere some clown had to recast my innocent life as a suburban father of three as something very different. How that guy took my life as a telecom CEO and convinced a grand jury I was the worst thing since Osama Bin Laden, I have no idea. But I may never know who did that to me, or if I have been the victim of the unintended consequences of targeting algorithms. That's impossible to know, at least at the moment.

Obviously I have certain libertarian leaning opinions regarding privacy, civil liberties, and criminal justice reform. I do not, however, hate those that disagree with me, nor do I see a need to demonize them. I accept the fact that not everyone has all the facts I do, or the free time to ponder these many issues. Sometimes people come up with the wrong answers for many reasons, and not everyone processes all the input logically, without emotion, politics, or greed factored in.

Amazingly, the government isn't required to use the Scientific Method for anything. Statistics are often totally ignored when they are inconvenient. And it's totally legal for government officials to make decisions based on religion, or social biases. Such is life, and it's not my place to change it. I accept the fact that the USA will likely never change, and will probably only get worse. All evidence points in that direction. With that in mind, I simply envision my personal future in another country.

In fact, if I was pardoned today, I'd simply leave the US and never return. I'd probably even quit writing about mass surveillance topics altogether, and focus on my fiction. But that's a highly unlikely scenario, and I don't spend a lot of time fantasizing about it. What I do focus on is becoming more informed and educated. If I have to sit in prison then I hope to at least enlighten a few people with my writing. If I can save one person from losing their freedom to the police state via my writing, then my time here isn't being wasted. And that, my friends, is my sole purpose in life at the moment.

Chapter 2: What is a Hacker?

In the early days the term "hacker" had a colloquial meaning that wasn't altogether disparaging. Since then the idealistic characteristics associated with the term seem to have faded. Back in the late 80's and early 90's there were few hackers of any public notoriety to really set a norm. Kevin Mitnick and Kevin Poulson's early exploits certainly didn't damage the image any; if anything they lived up to the stereo-type. Then there was the movie "Hackers" that was so far-fetched that anyone with any skills whatsoever cringed at the site of it. That being said, the soundtrack wasn't horrible. But somewhere along the way the term began to be used for a wider swath of characters.

Due to the increased availability of early Windows apps like Back Orifice, SubSeven, Brutus, and all manner of easy to use "hacking" utilities, cyber-attacks became more frequent. We could also assert that the bursting of the tech bubble put a lot of people with a certain set of skills out of work. Whatever the reason, the term hacker began to be associated with defacements (when a website is digitally vandalized), data theft, and data loss. This was probably equally the fault of those of us that were early to the "carding" scene as well. This was a critical juncture for the term, and someone failed society, and ruined it for the rest of us.

Someone, I'm not sure who, lacked the imagination to come up with a new term for an ethical network security professional, and so they just put a hat on the old term. It was then that the term "white hat" came into existence, forcing all of us that weren't engaged in Penetration Testing as a legal business to be "Black Hats". Let's set aside the fact that most of the "ethical" network security groups put money ahead of ethics. For the moment, we'll even pretend that all these groups keep up with the laws of every single country on the planet, and never play favorites. The mere existence of something called a white hat forced everyone into one camp or the other. Not literally of course, no one in the scene actually noticed or cared, but the media and the policy makers took the ball and ran with it.

The term white hat stuck, and became a part of the discussion. In my opinion this was the first blow to cyberanarchy, information freedom, and an open internet. With one little phrase, a cloak of criminality was draped over everyone that wasn't a card carrying white hat.

When I first saw the term white hat used online, my first thought was "coward". I don't understand why someone doing a network security job has to even be called a hacker. Why not "Network Security Analyst" instead? Clearly they want to keep the romantic idea of being a hacker, without any of the liability associated with the title. I mean ,I understand making a living doing network security testing, I can respect that in some tiny way. But the term seems to indicate that one's hands are tied by the title. It's to say: "I won't break the law", whatever that law may be, in whatever country, which is absurd. I mean if you represent a client that is getting port scanned daily from a Chinese IP address, one that's jumping around in a couple random subnets, a white hat could deploy a dozen honey pots in VPS (Virtual Private Servers) with IDS (Intrusion Detection Systems) to build an IP blacklist for null routing on the border router. Sure, that's just basic network security work. But does a white hat lose his white hat card for corrupting the firmware of some random Chinese router instead? If that's the cheapest and easiest solution, isn't it most ethical to tell your US client that's an option? Who's to say what is and isn't ethical at that point? Was there a committee meeting I didn't get invited to?

To be fair, a lot of the white hats sold the label to their probation officers first. It was a way for people with that certain set of skills to stay in the industry after a negative law enforcement encounter. That, and I expect a lot of active black hats have hid behind the veil of being in the business of ethical network security work. It's become a term of convenience for many.

Then there was the inevitable rise of the Gray Hat. Ostensibly this is what the original hackers were; those that just looked but didn't touch. Those that exploit networks just to do it, but didn't do any real damage or sell your data. The definition of each hat tends to vary online, and the media misuses every technical term that has anything to do with IT as it is. Thus, the confusion continues.

But for all my readers, here is a top secret hacker factoid you may find nowhere else: real hackers don't refer to themselves as hackers.

Seriously. Drug dealers generally don't refer to themselves as drug dealers either. These are all labels assigned by society outside the scene all to fit into the sound bites of modem media, and to give law enforcement some common vernacular.

I ran a black hat forum for years, and the terms "black hat" and "hacker" never appeared on the site. Hell, I didn't even think of it as a black hat site until the FBI referred to it with that label. From my perspective, I had a site for the discussion of exploits, tools, and technologies associated with network security (or lack thereof).

Maybe it sounds strange for a group of thousands of hackers to have never discussed being hackers, but that's just the way it was. In comparison, I doubt a lot of Eskimos are sitting around discussing being Eskimos either, or what particular kind of Eskimo they are. If had to guess, they probably spend a lot of time discussing the best holes to fish out of. Which is more or less what black hat groups do as well.

Now, I might be going out on a limb here, but I say I might be thought of by many as an authentic black hat hacker. I spent a year as an international fugitive being tracked by the FBI's Cybercrime Task Force and Interpol. I was eventually convicted of one of the largest domestic cybercrimes in US history. I received a 30 year prison sentence for this crime, and I was sent to federal prison, where I am now. I'm not sure what the actual qualifications for the job title are, but I think I might fit the bill better than anyone that did a year in a federal prison camp for "Access Device Fraud", or simple "Intrusion".

I'm also the former Chief Executive Officer of several multi-million dollar tech companies. For years, as an entrepreneur I wore many hats: network engineer, software designer, IT system manager, and others. A title I used often was: "Network Security Professional", but that title too fails to convey any meaningful information as to ethical leanings.

Plenty of those referred to as hackers are actually "script kiddies". These clowns tend to use Windows apps with a GUI, with no understanding of the underlying TCP/IP protocols, much less the IP Stack or Memory Management on their target machine. But to say "Network Security Professional", we could be referring to the FBI's Cybercrime task force itself, but they are completely useless without their software systems. I guess that makes them White Hat Script Kiddies. It turns out those with sufficient elite technical skills to have mastered all things IT rarely choose to work for a government for a small percentage of the money they'd make in the private sector.

I couldn't even have a conversation with the FBI without them flipping through Newton's Telecom Dictionary, and Google. It wasn't a debriefing, and it wasn't an interrogation. We couldn't have had a real conversation even if had wanted to (which I didn't). Hours of my life were wasted pretending to cooperate while sharing information that they could have found online anyway, but they needed someone to dumb it down for them. It was a brain-numbing and frustrating event that I forced myself to endure under advice of my attorney.

Every American should be terrified that the head of FBI's Cybercrime task force got his job because he was the only agent that knew how to install Windows on the day the task force was created. Is it any wonder that virtually every US government agency has been hacked? Hypothetically, if I wanted to hire a freelance Network Security Professional of some kind, I might search DICE, or Monster, but the resume highlights wouldn't be cut and dry. There would be those with an Associate's Degree in IT, with an MSCE certificate, that for all intents and purposes meets the minimum criteria for the job description. I'm sure his first client would see no cause for alarm when he booted Windows up on his Dell laptop and began loading a commercial exploit scanner.

Yet somewhere in an international airport right now at this very second, there sits a kid with Kali booted up on his laptop dumping packets to Wireshark and watching them go by. The kid could be from Estonia, and probably doesn't even have a degree. Nevertheless, he could pass the CCNA, CCNP, and the CCIE Cisco certification exams if he wanted to do so. And if he wanted to get into the network that the above mentioned MSCE is busy securing, it's going to happen. So who's the real Network Security Professional? For years I toiled away into the wee hours of the night in the glow of 6 stacked 24" LED monitors. I connected with a bonded Cisco 1700 series router with dual Cat6 lines to separate Verizon FiOS Optical Network Terminations. In spite of the above, my family had no idea I was any kind of hacker. And even when I was compiling exploits on remote servers, I myself didn't think of myself as a hacker.

When I wrote a script to check VoIP calls through a certain carrier with incrementing billing prefixes, I viewed that as "testing", and not "hacking". And when I used those found prefixes to exploit a carrier that had ripped off my company, it wasn't hacking to me, it was just business.

Later, as I sat in my orange jumpsuit in a Federal Courtroom while the FBI expounded on how dangerous I was, I didn't feel like a hacker then either. They used the word "cybercriminal" a lot actually, and made a very big deal out of the fact that I could apparently create my own fake ID. So apparently being proficient in Photoshop can make you a hacker as well.

Today there are all kinds of hackers. I recently read an article on a Green Hat hacker; basically a black hat but for a good cause, that being the environment. Why couldn't that guy just be an eco-terrorist, or a hacktivist? Did he really need his own colored hat? Worse yet, now the term is used in relationship to anyone that alters anything in some unconventional way. We have "gene hackers", and even "body hackers", although the latter sounds more like a B-movie that should have died with VHS.

With all the different kinds of hackers, the meaning of the term has become completely obscured and entirely subjective. I worry that the future generations will follow the lead of governments and view all cyber-nonconformist as criminals. Gone are the days of network exploration without consequences. Now you have to setup proxies, rent a VPS with a prepaid card, and do all the things criminals would do, just to run a port scan. For me, getting root after hours of work was like hitting the lotto. Even if the box only had a lame porn collection and some ass-hat's email, it was the thrill of the discovery that was its own reward. But I'm afraid that era has passed.

Movies like Swordfish, The Matrix, and others set the stage for the romantic ideal of what hacking was. In reality, the scene was much more subtle and nuanced, but no less exciting. It becomes a part of who you are. It alters how you look at the world around you. It's about looking at an instruction manual or white-paper and thinking "well that's a good start, but what if..." It's about those of us that understand there is no such thing as perfect network security, and why. It's human nature to want to understand how things work, and what the limits are. That's what the Science Technology Engineering and Mathematics (STEM) fields are for. But today, all that real world research has been criminalized. Since governments are now buying zero-day exploits with your tax dollars and weaponizing their own code, they certainly don't want any competition.

So here we are in a world that punishes people for their intellectual capacity, regardless of intent or any overt acts. It's become a liability to be known to have those certain skills. The powers that be want all their sheep to navigate the sausage factory without asking how any of the machinery works. Obviously I made a very bad sheep, a black one maybe, as here I am in federal prison. But does that make me a black hat hacker? If I repent, and swear off fuzzing, and spolitz, can I be forgiven by some almighty digital demigod that will then bestow upon me white hat status? Or is it once a black hat, always a black hat? I mean, can you go black, and go back? Now that everyone is a hacker of one kind or another, am I even a real hacker anymore? And what exactly is a real hacker? So this is quite the quandary, I, don't even know what to call myself. In a world that lets an MSCE be a "Network Security Professional", and a script kiddie be a "hacker". I'm not sure I want to be either one. And that is why I hate all the silly labels, and why I reject the very premise or such stereotyping. Yet here I am forced to wear the black hat, and be that guy nonetheless.

I know this isn't going to make a simple sound bite for the ADD generation, but until there is a good buzz word that best represents a truly evil radical-libertarian/cryptoanarchist/prolific-pirate/ network- security-engineer with the propensity for interstate flight to avoid prosecution, you can just refer to me as a black hat to keep it simple. Maybe I can take back the term. But if I am to be a black hat, let's discuss what a black hat is and is not.

Chapter 3: What is a Black Hat?

It would be easy to simply say that a black hat hacker is a criminal hacker. We could even say that any hacker that isn't a certified ethical "white hat" hacker must be a black hat. There is much debate as to what a black hat is and is not, often debated by the "is-nots". Since I'm someone that almost everyone can agree on is certainly a black hat, I feel obligated to describe the term in detail. Beyond the important description to follow, we also need to cover why it is that anyone should take security and privacy advice from such a character.

Upon finding $100 in the street some people would take the money to the local police department and report the discovery. We can all imagine what each of us would do in that situation. Logically our decision would be affected by how many people could see us pick up the money, the time of day, our bank balance, our hungry children, needy spouse, or personal sense of ethics. And all of that would be affected by the dollar amount found. A man might take a bank bag found with $5,000 in it, to the police department, and yet take a plastic bag with $30,000 in it home to announce new plans for a vacation with his wife. But the same man might skip out on the wife altogether and leave the country if he found $500,000. Such is humanity. We all have our moral, ethical, and personal codes which evolve with our wants and needs of the day.

To expand on the found-money analogy, obviously a farmer having just lost his farm to the bank is more likely to keep the bank bag found in the bank's parking lot. That doesn't mean the same farmer would rob that bank with a gun, or that he'd beat up a girl scout and take her cookie money. Unfortunately the label "black hat" is often conveyed in such a way to indicate that we would indeed punch that Girl Scout right in the face for a nickel since we are almost certainly going to get away with it hiding behind our proxies in some dark basement somewhere. That simply isn't true.

Like you, each of us has our price. For me, I'd never touch a working class citizen, or small business. In fact, when I found a security hole, I'd usually alert the business owner to the problem. I once got spam from a compromised server ran by a dental service. I called the owner on his personal mobile phone number to let him know there was a problem. He thought I was kidding until I read off his client's names and credit card numbers. Although I undoubtedly ruined the good dentist's evening, I felt morally obligated to point out the problem. That doesn't make me a white hat, or any kind of hero, it was just ten minutes out of my tens of thousands of hours online.

In another example, a large telecom company purchased a business division from my company. In this case it was a few hundred residential VoIP customers. For the uninitiated, that means customers that used the internet for their phone service, and that paid my company for the service. The contract said the telecom company would pay us out over 6 months on projected and realized revenue from the clients we sold them. We never got a dime. When I inquired about the lack of payment, their CEO said that they didn't fully convert as many of the customers as they had hoped on all of their up-sales. I referred to the contract which specified that wasn't an issue for non-payment. He said "So sue us". He knew that protracted litigation with his much larger company would be very costly for my company, and likely to be settled for far less than what he owed. In the business, this is called a "decision to litigate", and it's a tactic oft used in telecom.

Legally, ethically, and morally the FBI believes I should have simply let the lawyers deal with it. That's not what happened. Instead, I activated a shelf company, converted it into a virtual corporation, and purchased telecom service from the company that had screwed us. I signed up for 100 channels of "unlimited" long distance service, and flowed $1.1 million dollars' worth of wholesale long distance service from my network, into their network, all in a single weekend. By the time they checked their logs on Monday morning I had already sent hundreds of thousands of calls from a real-time telecom exchange service that uses a Least Cost Routing (LCR) matrix. Which means: whoever has the cheapest rate, gets to complete the call. It turns out I had the lowest rates for Afghanistan and Cuba for the whole weekend, at an average of over $0.50 a minute to those high-cost areas.

We can argue the ethics, but from my black hat perspective, it was justified. From the FBI's perspective, it was obviously illegal, as the fine print for their "unlimited plan" clearly said it wasn't really unlimited and was not to be used for wholesale traffic, or commercial use. How corporate contracts figure into criminal law would be another book entirely, but the gist of the idea is that the bigger company that pays more taxes is always right.

In my opinion, a black hat isn't intrinsically criminal or evil, maybe just more selectively opportunistic. If you're a gamer, you know that in the old Dungeons and Dragons role playing games, right up through current day RPG video games, you have a characteristic called "alignment". These are an assignment of code of ethics that the character plays, such as Lawful-Good, Evil-Bad, and my favorite Chaotic-Neutral. Although there is a such thing in the gaming world as Chaotic-Evil, it's my opinion that black hats are simply opportunistic, and thus Chaotic-Neutral.

For example, I keep found money, but I don't beat up girl scouts or small businesses. Although, it's said that I am a professional criminal, so maybe that it's just that I know Girl Scouts don't have millions of dollars I can steal in a weekend. So be it ethics, or just common sense, professional hackers that are engaged in cybercrime for a living tend to target bigger fish. Sure, some low level scofflaws will steal your grandmother's identity and use it in a Medicare scam. However that shouldn't define all black hats. That level of play is largely driven by regular criminals simply utilizing some aspects of technology, and not actual black hats.

Years ago I would have thrown all script kiddies under the bus, but today there are a few professional cybercriminals that can't code, and can't hack. These individuals use high end crimeware readily available on the dark web. It doesn't magically produce money though, it's just a tool. Those that have mastered these tools can do quite well for themselves. But as law enforcement has equal access to these same tools, a much higher percentage of the crimeware crowd ends up arrested than real black hats that can write their own code. Again, these script kiddies aren't black hats, but from the victims perspective that wouldn't matter much.

Black hats are network and/or software security professionals that first know how to code, and from that skill are able to glean illicit data to further their endeavors. Being able to see behind the scenes allows us to do things that wouldn't be possible otherwise.

Here's an example of a behind the scenes play that shows the value of illicit data, but with no coding required. Bank of America has pretty good security surrounding their commercial account access. However, there's nothing to prevent a bank employee from taking notes on what loan got approved versus denied. We used to pay a guy to send us snapshots of loan applications that were later approved by the bank's automated system. He blacked out the names, but that didn't matter.

From that little bit of information we were able to reverse engineer their automated approval algorithm for easy instant approvals for our shelf companies, ones that would not be forwarded to their human risk management teams. From there it was simply a matter of duplicating the approved company's stats with our shelf companies.

You will not need a bank insider to protect your finances from hackers or malevolent governments. What you do need is an understanding of how things work behind the scenes. That's the secret sauce. As I've spent years as a black hat, as a CEO, and now a convicted felon in the US federal prison system, I now have the full spectrum of perspective to report from.

It may seem opportunistic of me to talk to incarcerated hackers and then write a book on how they hide their money, and it is. Although, with the ones that got caught we are only extrapolating which trip wires they stepped on where. In most cases they were only caught by chance, or human stupidity, and weren't necessarily the victim of government seizures due to a complete failure of OpSec. Such as in my case, where I am alleged to have stolen $25,000,000. Although the FBI has searched for years now, they haven't recovered a dime. They did however give me an extra 10 years in prison for "Obstruction of Justice - Hiding Assets". Apparently there is a US law that says you are supposed to give up all your money to prevent an effective legal defense, and to ensure the effectiveness of the prosecution, regardless of actual guilt. Who knew?

But fear not, your money is your money, and it's not a crime to keep it. In my case they were really upset with me for reasons well beyond just the money. That being said, this book is of course not intended to replace good legal advice, nor is it constrained to a US-Only world-view. We assume that people all over the world want to protect their assets and conduct business with maximum privacy, and so please look elsewhere for legal advice for any one particular country.

I won't delve into the minutia of the US legal system, or my mistreatment by that thereof, that's irrelevant to the topic at hand. The goal here is to understand financial surveillance systems and black hat tradecraft, and the crimeware that can put your finances at risk. If you derive your wealth from hard work, criminal activity, or found money, it's no one's business but your own. It's all equally at risk when banked the old fashioned way under the watchful eye of governments, hackers, and even the script kiddies that have just purchased a "Crimeware for Dummies Kit" off the dark web.

Chapter 4: The Hacker Lingo

It would be impossible to write a book on this subject without using a little of the lingo hackers are famous for. It will not be necessary to learn "leetspeak", but you will need to learn a few terms of the trade. Although some of the vocabulary for black hat tradecraft certainly evolved out of intelligence agency vocabulary, the bulk of the lexicon developed in IRC channels, web forums, instant messaging, and blogs. Here you can find terms gleaned from leaked government documents within the conversations between hackers, right next to terms borrowed from science fiction and gaming. The hacker lingo is truly a unique and mercurial manifestation of the shared knowledge-base of the trade, and understandably difficult for those new to the subculture.

In fact, once I was forcibly removed from the online world of the dark arts, I found it difficult to even discuss technology with my lawyers. I had to create a cheat sheet just for them to read the many emails the government intended to use against me.

Reluctantly, I agree with my editor that writing a book in leetspeak would not appeal to the audiences we wish to reach with this book. Accordingly, all overtly technical terminology has been either avoided, or explained in detail within the context of the usage here. Otherwise I do use the lingo where it will save my dear reader time. For example, instead of saying "whoever it is that you feel you need to protect your money or data from", we say the "opposing force", abbreviated down to simply OpFor. These few terms are necessary to acquire contextually as they apply to your personal or professional situation.

There are undoubtedly well educated professionals from other fields reading this that feel it unnecessary to learn these "slang" terms, but consider the following. Human beings are merely biological machines running a highly adaptable operating system. Our neurological software isn't coded in Python, C, or the binary used in computers. We use language. English speakers borrow from other languages all the time. We get "faux paus" from the French, and that term is encoded in our gray matter and linked to all manner of memories and associations ready for use as needed. These new terms will help reshape your thinking as needed to become a successful and independent "operator", capable of managing your own "operational security", which will be necessary to protect yourself from the OpFor that have the potential to separate you from your wealth, identity, or freedom. If none of that makes sense to you yet, fear not, it will be explained shortly.

Chapter 5: Operators

In the wide world of cybercrime, law enforcement, intelligence gathering, big money, fast money, and with all things financially illicit, there are only two types of characters: operators, and potential victims. We could argue that law enforcement is a third class, but really they are just operators themselves, usually confined to a single team and level of play. In the case of dirty cops, such as the FBI agents charged with stealing BitCoins in the Silk Road case, we can see that operators are operators with or without a badge.

In another analogy, the US will refer to evil Russian hackers as the bad guy for any number of events. Yet you will never hear the American media refer to American hackers working for US intelligence agencies, the military, or law enforcement, mentioned as the bad guys. They can do no wrong. Yet to the Chinese and Russians, the US government hackers are the bad guys, and they certainly make the news in other countries. And so it is a very subjective reality in which one determines who is the good guy, or bad guy, but what's important here is not who's playing for which team, just that we identifier the players (the operators) versus the spectators (the victims). The key to being successful in the endeavors described in this book is protecting yourself from becoming a victim, by becoming an operator.

There has always been a class divide between the rich and the poor, and over the years we've seen the divide widen between the intelligentsia and the less gifted. It is said that in the future there will only be two types of jobs: those in which you tell robots what to do, and those in which you are told what to do by robots. Although I love the quote, I don't think it's entirely true. Obviously there will be more tech sector jobs in the future, and less in manufacturing, that's true. But it's not as simple as being intelligent, or being able to code, nor is success denied to those with neither trait nor ability. I assert that this is instead the precipice of the age of pure informational warfare, in which the winners and losers will be divided up by who controls the data: who has access to the best and most external data, while protecting their own.

In an extreme example, one could throw a national election with well placed "leaked" data. Well, maybe that's not that extreme, but we can all agree that political ambitions have been dismembered repeatedly by the disclosure of one bit of private data or another.

That's the big picture. On a more personal level, some one that keeps up with technology and their education will always have an advantage over those that waste the days of their lives watching reality television. As economies shift, that advantage will mean the difference between dire poverty and great wealth. Either way, these are not necessarily the lives of operators, just the passive observers waiting to become victims at different points in the food chain. Being an operator is another level entirely.

We've covered what a hacker is and is not. We've discussed the difference between black hats and white hats. But what is an operator? Although all operators are not black hats, any black hat that is making a dime from his trade is an operator. NSA and FBI agents are operators, cartel hit men are operators, and the Nigerian's that send you those phishing emails are also operators. It's not about legal or illegal, it's about those that are playing the game versus those that are sitting in the bleachers. Operators play an active role in their own security, wellbeing, and quality of life. To do that, they have to open up flows of information that help them insulate themselves from those that would put them at risk. For many of you, the first step in this process was the purchase of this book. It's generally not necessary to spend your entire day reading network security white papers. You do not need a degree in computer science, or a brother-in-law that works for the NSA, or for Geek Squad. If you are a full time cybercriminal with your name on a Red Notice in INTERPOL, then you might want to make security a life's endeavor, and quit using that name obviously.

For most people it's simply a matter of developing a basic understanding of the technology that you depend on in life, and what your OpFor is capable of. That's how you begin a life as an operator.

The next step is making the lifestyle choice to take your personal security into your own hands. Operators do not subcontract their safety and security to others, or rely on the nanny state to protect them. First world governments are fair weather friends at best. The US throws veterans under the bus, incarcerates the mentally ill, and will freeze all your assets for the slightest tax anomaly. To rely on "the government" to protect your money or your data is an exercise in delayed disappointment. Are you within the.001 % of the US population that does everything by the book, documents everything, pays 100% of the taxes possible, and never encroaches upon any of the 20,000 pages of US criminal law? If not, then using a personal bank account in the US is the same as setting up a savings account for the government to take later. Eventually the FBI's case management system will vector your name in their database, and if you score high enough, or some case agent has to hit their quota, bad things happen.

If their algorithm says Bill has $20,000 in a bank account, or Bill put $100,000 in some combination of bank accounts over a year's time, but Bill reported less than $100,000 on his personal tax return, then that's a red flag. Thinking the US government doesn't monitor all banking transactions is an act of desperate optimism. The golden rule of OpSec is: Optimism is NOT a security policy. They factor in PayPal, eTrade, and even your personal credit report. If you report making $40,000 a year to the IRS, but make more than that in car and house payments, your days are numbered.

Concerning optimism, you thinking you are doing everything right is only an effective strategy if you truly know and understand all the law and the tax code, otherwise you have very obvious exposure. Information is key, but no human can truly know all the laws of any first world nation. Conspiracy theorists and quite a few law professors would argue that is by design. The only solution is to take control of your own data, and manage your own security. In later chapters we'll cover the litany of actions that can get someone vectored by a government, or that can make them easy prey for hackers.

For understanding what and operator is or is not, the key here is that operators are actively managing their "operations security". Everyone else is just letting life happen to them while engaged in desperate optimism devoid of the slightest inkling of statistical analysis. The odds on passive success are astronomically improbable. Millions of identities are stolen every year. Even the biggest companies you entrust your data with get hacked all the time, as did Target, TJ Max, and Yahoo. The banks themselves have proven that they too will game your data, as did Wells Fargo with their new account scandal. Meanwhile, the US Office of Personnel Management was hacked, so the keys to the castle are already in the hands of black hats. These are just a few of the stories that made the national main stream media in the US. We already know the vast majority of hacks, government abuses, and corporate mismanagement cases go unreported. You simply can't afford to trust your security to a 3rd party. We'll discuss how to maintain personal and professional OpSec in coming chapters.

Let's look at a few examples of operators:

1) At one end of the spectrum we have an operator like Jim who works for a big company and augments his salary with a kickback from a vendor every now and then. Not every vendor, not every time, but a couple of vendors he knows personally in which case he was responsible for the business relationship's creation between the vendor, and his employer. Jim keeps a separate offshore account for these funds, and he's taken steps to isolate his banking tools to prevent commingling of the accounts.

Is that illegal? Generally only if you are a public official, otherwise it's likely only a violation of Jim's employment policy. In some countries it's pretty much the norm, but in the US it seems to be a firing offense. Is it ethical? That's a subjective call that would be based on Jim's employee/ employer relationship. Regardless, Jim is an operator, and he's in control of his financial situation. On paper he gets paid from his company, has his taxes taken out, and in all databases he looks as he should. However, with the offshore account, he can take extra payments, and build up a nice retirement package for himself free and clear of any risk of a 3rd party managed 401K, or government approved retirement plan.

2) Bob is an operator that runs a legal marijuana retail outlet in a state where it's legal by state law. He sells internationally via the mail, and can't accept payment in the US and pay taxes on the sales because of the federal prohibition on marijuana. Which I might add, is going far worse than the last attempt at prohibition with alcohol. A bit of history for you, that failed attempt to regulate personal freedoms was responsible for the creation of the Mexican cartels. Yes, they go that far back, and when alcohol became legal again, they switched to drugs, and as we can see, they've done quite well for themselves. But back to Jim, he takes payment via BitCoin on the dark web, and uses local Bit coin sales to make cash available to reinvest in his business. Is that legal? Hell if I know.

Is it ethical? Research has shown that the chemicals in marijuana have a variety of medicinal uses, including preventing seizures in children in cases where no other prescribed medication has proven effective. The chemicals in marijuana have shown great promise in the treatment of a number of serious medical disorders, but not much in the US. In the US the drug is so heavily regulated that research is all but fully suppressed, and thus the bulk of the research is taking place outside of US jurisdiction. Meanwhile, it's available throughout the US and in any high school in America. A conspiracy theorist might suggest that Big Pharma played a role in suppressing legalization, but it's a fact that the cigarette and alcohol companies are against legalization.

The question is, should we allow a government of one country to deny someone outside their jurisdiction access to these substances merely because the government doesn't have the political will to accept 30 years of failed drug policy?

Politicians don't read statistics, they are often blind to all the facts, but wide open to lobbyists. And if you don't think their decisions are based on the will and force of big corporate lobbyists rather than the will of the people, then can I interest you in an unhackable laptop with a fresh installation of Windows XP? Maybe the worst part of being a black hat and spending so much time reading other people's email on corporate servers is that you quickly realize that there simply is little or no goodwill in corporate America, and that there is a dark side to capitalism that is kept from the general public.

An aside, although I mention marijuana in examples here, I do not suggest the use of any drug that doesn't make you faster, stronger, or smarter. Marijuana will in no way, shape, or form improve one's ability to stay ahead of hackers or evil governments. In fact, the buying or selling or any illegal drugs merely increases your risk of getting vectored, and it gives the government a free pass to take every dime you have. But personally I think it should be legal in the US, if for no other reason than to prevent it from being used as the go-to strategy for the instant seizures of accounts and assets.

3) Lisa is planning on retiring in the next few years. She has good credit in the US that she knows will be worthless outside the country. She also knows her money will go much further in the Caribbean, where the quality of life is higher, and the cost of living far lower. Lisa decides to prepare an exit strategy. As an operator, she begins setting up offshore accounts in Offshore Financial Centers (OFC), and migrating her savings out of the US without tax exposure using a pair of virtual corporations. She plans to ramp up her personal credit to personally guarantee a large corporate loan

before leaving.

Is it ethical to take out a loan you have no intentions of repaying? No, it isn't. Is it legal? Technically no, but the issue at that point is "badges of fraud". This is a legal term that defines conditions for intent to defraud, and intent is required for the law to be broken. But thousands of companies in the US go under all the time, so the difference between bad business and fraud is only the intent, the results are the same for the creditors.

As long as Lisa operated independently and never told anyone her intent, it would be impossible to prosecute. For that reason it's extremely rare for law enforcement to step in where corporate debt is concerned, and generally only in cases where there are single "acts of fraud" in excess of $100,000. I learned this the hard way when I called the FBI myself the first time a client's corporation ripped off my company. I called the FBI myself, and they couldn't have been less interested.

The Dallas FBI office specifically told me that the US Attorney (federal prosecutor) would only be interested in pursuing cases if they exceeded $100,000, and still only if there was some evidence of fraud versus just corporate debt gone bad. To which I said, "So I can get ripped off for millions as long as it's in smaller chunks?" You wouldn't believe the slick non-answers the FBI has on the screens of their inbound call center. The short of it is, if it's corporate debt, then they don't have the resources to police contract law unless you are a big company they are in bed with, or unless it can be a slam dunk and/or show piece case for the US Attorney's office. Sadly, this lack of policing has encouraged all manner of bad capitalism in certain sectors. And yes, I myself, a criminal, is complaining about the FBI's lack of policing. It's that bad. Meanwhile, the prisons are full of people that merely introduced two people that later sold each other drugs. Only in the US of A can you find this insanity.

With that in mind, if Lisa was to take on dozens of smaller loans and leases, and make payments for 6 months or so, her data would later look no different than any other failed business. Maybe Lisa wants to start an orphanage in Guatemala to help impoverished children. Maybe she wants a condo on the beach in Antigua. Whatever the reason, anyone on her path is considered an operator.

4) In a more obvious case, Sean the black hat hacker wears a nice suit and has a website that details his employment as a

technology consultant. He travels the planet on multiple passports linked to citizenship in a half dozen different countries. In each of those countries he owns real-estate, and he has a lawyer on retainer. Most of Sean's clients are big evil corporations, or organized crime, and he's got the best James Bond gadgets money can buy. Sean can code in a dozen programming languages, and he's fluent in three languages. This is not the level you need to reach to be an operator, but people like Sean exist and they can and will rob your bank, PayPal, or eTrade account if they are so inclined. To protect yourself from an indirect attack by such an operator, you may only need to appear as something more complex than merely the low hanging fruit for an easy hack. Better yet, don't appear at all.

5) Herbert is an FBI analyst, and his job is to do what his computer tells him to do. Running advanced heuristic algorithms the FBI Case Management System (CMS) pulls data from the National Criminal Information Center (NCIC), the credit bureaus, court filings, social media, the IRS, motor vehicle registrations, and over 150 other sources. This system sorts, rates, and scores people for the FBI's investigation. There is heavily weighted input from intelligence agencies as well, with links to Call Detail Records (CDR) from the NSA's access to telecom companies, and Internet Service Providers (ISP) customer databases. If a person has a lot of complaints from the general public, their score increases, but that is a far lower scoring variable than many of the others. If the person represents a greater threat to government interest due to military experience, education, or outspoken political views, then their score is increased. But most of all, if they appear to have reached their apex of criminality, and hence their point of maximum seizure value, they shoot to the top of the list.

In War World II the US developed sea mines that would sense a ship nearby via magnetism and sound, and not detonate when it was detected, but to wait until the signal started to diminish, as that was the apex of proximity. This basic algorithm runs on simple high school calculus, and could be coded on a personal calculator from 1991. There's nothing to it, especially now with cloud computing, and advanced machine learning. This process is fully automated, and fed by all US and allied intelligence agencies. Herbert's only real job is to check out the targets selected by the system and make sure they aren't otherwise working for the government in some capacity.

Beyond that, a case agent may be assigned to groom the selected target.

Typically in this situation a prospective target will undergo some actual investigation. The goal is to see if the target has any cash, real-estate, vehicles, or expensive toys that haven't already been considered in the algorithm. This is necessary, because apparently some people hide their assets. Go figure. Once this information comes back, it's loaded into the CMS for rescoring. FBI agents simply work on the top 50 cases based on this system and their available resources in the intended victims' area. The algorithm used by the FBI CMS is not visible to the FBI agents, much less the target. The code is adjusted based on the politics of the day, budgets, and public perception. Following the unrest in Ferguson, Missouri, in 2015, regular police officers who would have never been charged with civil rights violations before, suddenly found themselves at the top of the FBI's targeting system.

Thus public perception is weighted heavily, regardless of the fact that police officers tazering citizens is not exactly the biggest problem in America, nor is it profitable for seizures.

In my own federal case, the FBI didn't really care about corporate warfare between multi-million dollar telecom companies, until we displaced an NSA surveillance platform. Then I shot to the top of the list for targeting. The US federal government spent over $65 million dollars prosecuting our case, in which we had allegedly defrauded the telecom giants out of $25 million dollars. Obviously our encroachment upon the DEA's golden goose (their real-time access to phone calls to and from Mexico) earned our companies some bonus points in the FBI's system.

Although in this example case Herbert is an operator in his professional capacity, and here he represents the biggest threat to wealth, personally he's of little concern. The big problem is the targeting algorithm. In theory, the algorithm is only supposed to pick people for attention. The problem is that it's too easy for individual agents to become fully dependent on this all-knowing system that does much of their job for them, and the government is willfully blind to this condition as it benefits their seizure operations, and keeps the conviction rate up, as 95% of US defendants take a plea; it's an easy process.

As the code being used is of course entirely secret from the public, and the agents themselves, it would be hard to protect yourself against it. At least it would have been, had black hats like myself not spent decades refining techniques to reverse engineer algorithms such as those used by the FBI for targeting.

When hacking Wi-Fi hackers accumulate "hints" when connected devices continuously verify they are working with the same algorithm and key within their encryption scheme. This is how WEP connected devices stay connected. The way to crack WEP encryption is to accumulate thousands of these hints by collecting passing packets. Ostensibly these hints verify that every device on the network, connected to the Wireless Access Point (WAP), are authorized via the secret key. They don't send the key through the air, just mathematical hints that could only come from the same key. There's no way to resolve the key with just a single hint, or even a hundred of them, but once you have 40,000 to 80,000 of these using a decent computer (or passing the full package to Amazon's cloud computing platform, it's easy to resolve the key in seconds). This is a real example of the reverse engineering of an algorithm as used by black hats, and how the open source WEP Cracker tool works.

Similarly, the FBI's algorithm was reverse engineered, and there is an app running 24/7 today that absorbs new data and refines that algorithm. The raw code for this app is shared among criminal organizations, and it's been adapted for other governments using similar targeting algorithms. With it, sophisticated transnational criminal syndicates can stay just below radar, and maximize profits. Today, a cannibalized version of this code is used to target civilians and corporations for hacking as well. Understanding the simple elements that position your data within these algorithms is key to becoming a successful operator, and the prevention of becoming a victim of such technology.

Job one of any operator is to act and think like you are filling out a row in a database with everything you do. Thinking about how that data will be compared to your other rows in those databases is the best strategy for privacy and security. That, and you need to understand who your personal opposition may be, and what they are capable of.

Chapter 6: Opposing Force (OpFor)

In the discussion of protecting your wealth and financial data it's necessary to determine who or what it is that you are protecting yourself from. Let's assume you are a law abiding citizen that pays taxes, keeps all your records in order, and in no way, shape, or form ever does anything your government wouldn't approve of now, or in the future. That's a tall order, but I have met such super patriots that are on Team America regardless of what their government does to the rest of the planet. The joke in my sphere of international crime is that these are the people that took the blue pill with a tall glass of red, white, and blue Kool Aid. But that's okay, some people need to be on a team, and need to be told what to do, and in this case your opposing force (OpFor) would be evil hackers and transnational criminal organizations who would like to steal your identity and financial data to sell it for some trivial amount of money. I'm personally not a fan of identity theft, but it's a part of the business.

If you are not a US citizen, and you live outside the US, be advised that there are dozens of companies that provide financial surveillance platforms and monitoring systems to governments around the world. Even Mexico has been caught monitoring their citizens' phone traffic without a warrant. Government surveillance is becoming the new normal. So in almost every scenario, if you don't physically live in an Offshore Financial Center (OFC, a politically correct euphemism for "tax haven"), then a government is potentially an opposing force that can threaten your financial privacy and security. The US government is the most obvious clear and present danger to anyone that lives in the US, does business with the US, or does business with any of the many countries on the list of anti-American nation states. The US can force a European bank to freeze the assets of anyone doing business with Iran, or whoever it is this week that has resisted America's one-size-fits-all "democracy in a box" plan. I'm quoting a US general's pre-Iraq II invasion plan there, but it seems like western style democracy is often euphemistic for "puppet government".

Regardless of the politics, for those of us listening to the networks when there is a US sponsored change of leadership, the economic indicators are always visible well ahead of any media coverage of military bombings. There's a lengthy list of "private" companies that are either the benefactors or beneficiaries of US foreign policy adventures. These suits tend to show up as harbingers of things to come, and it's not clear if these are merely operators chasing wealth, or the US Central Intelligence Agency's (CIA) advanced guard. I'll leave that to the conspiracy theorists to debate, for our purposes here, you can assume they are both.

Above all else, remember "Optimism is not a Security Policy". Assume the worst, and use that as an opportunity to practice good security. Base you're planning on what's technically possible, and not what governments admit to doing that week. And never say it could never happen to you. Know the stats, and plan accordingly. If it's highly unlikely, allocate resources accordingly, but never bet your life, your freedom, or your wealth on the worst case scenario not happening. Work with the available data, use the techniques found in this book, but never forget that you will never have all the data. Plan for unknown variables, and have a backup plan. That's the very core of Operational Security (OpSec), which we'll get to in detail in a moment.

Concerning the OpFor, the bad news is and will continue to be, the more money you have, the more hands come out to get it. Operators working for governments or criminal organizations represent different threats, but that's only visible in the style of attack, not degree. Some work under the color of law, and some work from behind borders and proxies. Either can be very effective at ruining your life. Protect yourself accordingly. Start by determining who your OpFor might be; primary, secondary, and so forth.

Chapter 7: Operational Security (OpSec)

Before we can even begin to discuss the techniques to ensure financial privacy and security, we need to cover Operational Security. This means securing the perimeter of your endeavors. The perimeter in this case is the barrier between information only you know, and have access to, and the external world. Let's breeze through the basics: use good passwords, don't give your ATM PIN to strippers. Sorry, I mean "exotic dancers". And never answer those emails from Nigerian princes that need your banking info to help get their millions out of their country. Now, if it was only just that easy. Unfortunately things are a bit more complicated than that. This is where I have to plug another author's material.

For the absolute basics of OpSec I suggest "The Art of Invisibility" by Kevin Mitnick. His book is about basic OpSec in the modern world, and although I don't think it goes far enough for an operator, if you don't know a good password from a bad one, his book is a good starting point. Most of the material should be common sense, but if you are not very technical, then his book will help you get there. Here we'll lay out a road map for safe and secure techniques for banking, but we do so with the assumption that you at least know the basics of how to use a computer safely. Otherwise, you might want to pick up Kevin's book.

Throughout this book we'll cover the dos and don'ts of operational security, hereafter referred to as OpSec. At the core of OpSec is the simple premise that you and you alone control your financial data. In cases where we must use an offshore law firm, banks, brokers, and even unsecure Wi-Fi, there is a right way and many wrong ways to manage your OpSec, which we'll discuss in the coming chapters. The most common mistake is to trust a business partner, spouse, or romantic interest. To trust any human is to put your wealth on the roulette wheel of human emotions. For example, do you need to "buy" trust by giving a spouse access to a joint checking account? Fine, put in the minimum you can afford to lose and still buy that trust. Putting a dime more than you have to is an unnecessary risk, and understand that you are indeed just buying trust.

OpSec is about isolating risks, and limiting exposure. We do this by first eliminating all extraneous an unnecessary human interaction where security or finance is concerned. Naturally there is some part of the human ego that wants other people to believe we are smart, resourceful, and successful. That part of you will want to tell your spouse, business partner, or co-worker all about your offshore accounts and virtual currency usage. Somewhat ironically, this ego driven desire to appear smart, is in actuality an exercise in the demonstration of stupidity. There just isn't a pretty euphemism for stupid in this case, and so we must call it for what it is.

If you have any legal exposure you need to understand that law enforcement will interrogate everyone you know once you have been vectored for investigation. Even if your lovely spouse would never tell the government anything, it's enough that they simply know that they are lying for you. My wife was once charged with perjury in just such an occasion, and later sentenced in federal court for this felony count. Law enforcement receives training in detecting deception, and it's really quite easy. Most professional black hats have studied all the same interrogation manuals used by the FBI, and US Military. Little things like body language, eye movement, and the usage of conjunctions all point towards truthfulness or deception.

The psychological details of interrogation are beyond the scope of this book, but the point is that law enforcement personnel are usually really good at assessing deception. If you haven't trained to deceive, they will know when you are lying to them. It's what they do, and some do it quite well. You can generally depend on Law Enforcement being not very tech savvy in general, and totally checked out on Computer Science. If they had high level educations in neuroscience, machine learning, or network packet analysis, they wouldn't be working in law enforcement for a trivial paycheck. But where interrogations are concerned, that's their bread and butter, and as easy as it is, you can bet on them knowing it.

This isn't about trust. I trust my children to never do anything that would put me at risk, intentionally. But knowing they do not have counter-interrogation training, I'm not ever going to give them access to my BitCoin keys. In place of trust, we use solid OpSec.

We all know better than to give the keys of a new Ferrari to a 16 year old. That's simply irresponsible. Entrusting information regarding your offshore banking, virtual corporations, or cryptocurrency to your secretary, spouse, or anyone that doesn't have a pressing need to be intimately involved in your finances, is equally irresponsible. You put those people at risk by entrusting them with the information, and you create access points for exploitation by the OpFor. In the case of law enforcement, that could mean time in prison for your loved ones. In the case of organized crime, that can mean the loss of fingers, teeth, and toes.

Although it should be obvious that if it's not okay to share your data with one person, it's certainly not okay to share it with two. This bears exploration. In a scenario where your lawyer, your spouse, and business partner has access to your data, when something happens, who do you blame? That scenario is a recipe for disaster, as just when you need to depend on someone the most, you effectively lose your whole inner-circle, and risk falling back on the very traitor that robbed you to begin with. Keeping your data personal is the only solution. If you worry about being in the hospital, dying, or any of those situations where you'd want your family to have access to your otherwise hidden money, there are technical ways to deal with that. One such means is to put parts of keys in different spots, such as safety deposit boxes outside the US, or in paperwork filed with offshore attorneys. Although I favor the extreme personally. I like to hide encrypted data online.

For the first time ever I am going to now describe where my BitCoin keys are hidden. I like to embed keys in obscure pornography, right in the "JPG" file. I don't have to keep up with where it is stored, because I can rely on the internet as a whole to copy and paste that image millions of times and so it will always be available to me in the future. That, and I memorize my keys, and tend to save things on ruggedized USB drives, and then hide them in the ocean at memorized GPS coordinates. I find humans have great spacial memory, so I will remember those rocks on the ocean floor forever, but I have to rely on memory tricks to memorize the lengthy keys mnemonically.

The finer points of proper OpSec could fill their own book, but for our purposes here we'll cover the basics of OpSec as they relates to securing your finances. The tactics and techniques outlined here are used successfully by operators around the globe, but all the security apparatus comes unraveled the moment you allow another human access to your data. We can certainly secure our relationships with lawyers, bankers, and introduction services. That's covered fairly easily. Its personal relationships that are the bane of any operator. I've long since lost count of the number of times where I have heard the tales of woe beginning and ending with a failure of personal trust, which led to the loss of great wealth and freedom.

In order to become a successful operator it's necessary to assess OpSec decisions logically, with a pragmatic approach minus any silly emotional thoughts. It would be easy to use your offshore white-card Visa to pay for something online to be delivered to your home address. If this is an expense account you have setup as a slush fund for toys and luxuries, that's fine.

However, if you were to use a card linked to where the bulk of your liquid capital is, then you have exposed the location of your account and linked yourself to it. Even if you only used the card for iTunes, a federal agent can subpoena all the payment info associated with an iTunes account from Apple instantly via the handy portal Apple setup for speedy fed access. To start that process they could seize your iPhone of course, but it's just as easy for them to login to their portal with AT&T or Verizon to check and see if you have an iTunes account, and then go from there. It's a well-known fact that judges rubber-stamp warrant request of this nature, and I am personally convinced that it's only done after-the-fact in most cases, based on my years of research and experience. In my federal case there are dozens of documents that have dates marking their introduction into evidence that pre-date the warrant.

If your OpFor is intelligence agencies or hackers, a simple brush pass near your phone can facilitate a Near Field Communication (NFC), or Bluetooth attack. Easier yet would be a Man-in-the-Middle (MitM) attack between your phone and the cell tower or Wi-Fi hot spot. That happens. Governments use commercial "Stingray" devices for this purpose, and these devices can be easily constructed by hackers as well.

Assume anything in your phone can be exposed if it's ever used in the US, UK, Australia, New Zealand, or Canada. These are the "Five Eye" countries covered in the NSA documents leaked by Edward Snowden. These countries share intelligence, and use similar surveillance platforms due to common vendors. Although every country on Earth isn't interested in the minutia of their citizens' activities, if your risk factor is high enough, assume the limits of technology are in play, and plan accordingly.

You don't need to know the intricacies of telecommunications to protect yourself from this technology. If you bank in Dubai, Hong Kong, or Switzerland for your big money don't use that same account for daily transactions. Ideally, you'll have multiple accounts setup for different purposes, as I'll detail in upcoming chapters. There are dozens of ways to establish secure and anonymous banking relations abroad, but all is for not if you expose that information in person or electronically. Tight OpSec prevents exposure.

Chapter 8: The Eternal Value of Privacy

Each of us places a different value on privacy. When you read about these sweeping surveillance systems, you have to ask yourself why some people place so little value on privacy that they could let this happen.

The most common retort against privacy advocates by those in favor of ID checks, cameras, giant databases, data mining, and other wholesale surveillance measures is this line: "If you aren't doing anything wrong, what do you have to hide?"

Some clever answers to that are:
If I'm not doing anything wrong, then why watch me?
Because the government defines what's right and wrong, and they keep changing the definition.
Because you might do something wrong with my information.

My problem with quips like these, as right as they are, is that they accept the premise that privacy is about hiding a wrong. It's not. Privacy is an inherent human right, and a requirement for maintaining the human condition with dignity and respect. Two proverbs say it best: "Quis custodiet custodes ipsos?" ("Who watches the watchers?", and "Absolute power corrupts absolutely."

Cardinal Richelieu understood the value of surveillance when he famously said: "If one would give me six lines written by the hand of the most honest man, I would find something in them to have him hanged." Watch someone long enough, and you'll find something to arrest them for, blackmail them with.

Privacy is important because without it, surveillance information will be abused: to peep, to sell to marketers, and to spy on political enemies whoever they happen to be at the time.

Privacy protects us from abuses by those in power, even if we're doing nothing wrong at the time of surveillance. We do nothing wrong when we make love or go to the bathroom. We are not deliberately hiding anything when we seek out private places for reflection or conversation. We keep private journals, sing in the privacy of the shower, and write letters to secret lovers and then burn them. Privacy is a basic human need. A future in which privacy would face constant assault was so alien to the framers of the US Constitution that it never occurred to them to call out privacy as an explicit right. Privacy was inherent to the nobility of their being and their cause. Of course being watched in your own home was unreasonable. Watching at all was an act so unseemly as to be inconceivable among gentlemen in their day. You ruled your own home. It's intrinsic to the concept of liberty.

For if we are observed in all matters, we are constantly under threat of correction, judgment, criticism, and even plagiarism of our own uniqueness. We become children, fettered under watchful eyes, constantly fearful that either now, or in the uncertain future, patterns we leave behind will be brought back to implicate us, by whatever authority has now become focused upon our once private and innocent acts. We lose our individuality, because everything we do is observable and recordable.

How many of us have paused during conversation in the past few years, suddenly aware that we might be eavesdropped on? Probably it was a phone conversation, although maybe it was an e-mail or instant-message exchange, or a conversation in a public place. Maybe the topic was terrorism, politics, or Islam. We stop suddenly, momentarily afraid that our words might be taken out of context, then we laugh at our paranoia and go on. But our demeanor has changed, and our words are subtly altered.

This is the loss of freedom we face when our privacy is taken from us. This is life in former East Germany, or life in Saddam Hussein's Iraq. And it's our future as we allow an ever-intrusive eye into our personal, private lives. Too many wrongly characterize the debate as "security versus privacy." The real choice is liberty versus control. Tyranny, whether it arises under threat of foreign physical attack or under constant domestic authoritative scrutiny, is still tyranny. Liberty requires security without intrusion, security plus privacy.

Widespread police surveillance is the very definition of a police state. And that's why we should champion privacy even when we have nothing to hide.

Chapter 9: Something to Hide

Years ago surveillance programs like Carnivore, Echelon, and Total Information Awareness helped spark a surge in electronic privacy awareness. Now a decade later, the recent discovery of programs like PRISM, Boundless Informant, and rubber-stamped FISA orders are catalyzing renewed concern.

The programs of the past can be characterized as "proximate" surveillance, in which governments attempted to use technology to directly monitor communication themselves. The programs of this decade mark the transition to "oblique" surveillance, in which governments more often just go to the places where information has been accumulating on its own, such as email providers, search engines, social networks, and telecoms, collecting the data en masse for processing.

Both then and now, privacy advocates typically come into conflict with a persistent tension in which many individuals don't understand why they should be concerned about surveillance if they have nothing to hide. It's even less clear in the world of oblique surveillance, given that apologists will always frame our use of information gathering services like a mobile phone plan or Gmail as a choice. We are all viewed as potentially one big criminal conspiracy.

As James Duane, a professor at Regent Law School, and former defense attorney, notes in his excellent lecture on why it is never a good idea to talk to the police: estimates of the current size of the body of federal criminal law vary. It has been reported that the Congressional Research Service cannot even count the current number of federal crimes. These laws are scattered in over 50 titles of the United States Code, encompassing roughly 27,000 pages. And each year, law makers of course add new laws to the books; it's what they do.

Worse yet, the statutory code sections often incorporate by reference, the provisions and sanctions of administrative regulations promulgated by various regulatory agencies under congressional authorization. Estimates of how many such regulations exist are even less well settled, but the American Bar Association (ABA) thinks there are "nearly 10,000."

If the federal government can't even count how many laws there are, what chance does an individual have of being certain that they are not acting in violation of one of them? As Supreme Court Justice Breyer elaborated: "The complexity of modern federal criminal law, codified in several thousand sections of the United States Code and the virtually infinite variety of factual circumstances that might trigger an investigation into a possible violation of the law, make it difficult for anyone to know, in advance, just when a particular set of statements might later appear (to a prosecutor) to be relevant to some such investigation."

For instance, did you know that it is a federal crime to be in possession of a lobster under a certain size? It doesn't matter if you bought it at a grocery store, if someone else gave it to you, if it's dead or alive, if you found it after it died of natural causes, or even if you killed it while acting in self-defense. You can go to jail because of a lobster.

If the federal government had access to every email you've ever written and every phone call you've ever made, it's almost certain that they could find something you've done which violates a provision in the 27,000 pages of federal statues or 10,000 administrative regulations. This technique is used every day to prosecute federal defendants, generally regardless of actual guilt or innocence.

You probably do have something to hide, you just don't know it yet. Over the past year, there have been a number of headline grabbing legal changes in the US, such as the legalization of marijuana in many states, as well as the legalization of same-sex marriage in a growing number of US states.

As a majority of people in the United States apparently favor these changes, advocates for the US democratic process cite these legal victories as examples of how the system can provide real freedoms to those who engage with it through lawful means. And it's true, the bills did pass. What's often overlooked, however, is that these legal victories would probably not have been possible without the ability to break the law to begin with. The state of Minnesota, for instance, legalized same-sex marriage this year, but sodomy laws had effectively made homosexuality itself completely illegal in that state until 2001.

Likewise, before the recent changes making marijuana legal for personal use in WA and CO, it was obviously not legal for personal use. Imagine if there were an alternate dystopian reality where law enforcement was 100% effective, such that any potential law

74

offenders knew they would be immediately identified, apprehended, and jailed.

If perfect law enforcement had been a reality in MN, CO, and WA since their founding in the 1850s, it seems quite unlikely that these recent changes would have ever come to pass. How could people have decided that marijuana should be legal, if nobody had ever used it? How could states decide that same sex marriage should be permitted, if nobody had ever seen or participated in a same sex relationship?

The cornerstone of liberal democracy is the notion that free speech allows us to create a marketplace of ideas, from which we can use the political process to collectively choose the society we want.

Most critiques of this system tend to focus on the ways in which this marketplace of ideas isn't totally free, such as the ways in which some actors have substantially more influence over what information is distributed than others.

The more fundamental problem, however, is that living in an existing social structure creates a specific set of desires and motivations in a way that merely talking about other social structures never can. The world we live in influences not just what we think, but how we think, in a way that a discourse about other ideas isn't able to. Any teenager can tell you that life's most meaningful experiences aren't the ones you necessarily desired, but the ones that actually transformed your very sense of what you desire.

We can only desire based on what we know. It is our present experience of what we are and are not able to do that largely determines our sense for what is possible. This is why same sex relationships, in violation of sodomy laws, were a necessary precondition for the legalization of same sex marriage. This is also why those maintaining positions of power will always encourage the freedom to talk about ideas, but never to act. Law enforcement used to be harder. If a law enforcement agency wanted to track someone, it required physically assigning a law enforcement agent to follow that person around. Tracking everybody would be inconceivable, because it would require having as many law enforcement agents as people.

Today things are very different. Almost everyone carries a tracking device (their mobile phone) at all times, which reports their location to a handful of telecoms, which are required by law to provide that information to the government. Tracking everyone is no longer inconceivable, and is In fact, happening all the time. We know that Sprint alone responded to 8 million law enforcement requests for real time customer location just in 2008. They got so many requests that they built an automated system to handle them.

Combined with ballooning law enforcement budgets, this trend towards automation, which includes things like license plate scanners and domestically deployed drones, represents a significant shift in the way that law enforcement operates. Police already abuse the immense power they have, but if everyone's every action were being monitored, and everyone technically violates some obscure law at some time, then punishment becomes purely selective. Those in power will essentially have what they need to punish anyone they'd like, whenever they choose, as if there were no rules at all.

Even ignoring this obvious potential for new abuse, it's also substantially closer to that dystopian reality of a world where law enforcement is 100% effective, thus eliminating the possibility of experiencing alternative ideas that might better suit us.

Some will say that it's necessary to balance privacy against security, and that it's important to find the right compromise between the two. Even if you believe that, a good negotiator doesn't begin a conversation with someone whose position is at the exact opposite extreme by leading with concessions. And that's exactly what we're dealing with. Not a balance of forces which are looking for the perfect compromise between security and privacy, but an enormous steam roller built out of careers and billions in revenue from surveillance contracts and technology. To negotiate with that, we can't lead with concessions, but rather with all the opposition we can muster. **All the opposition we can muster!**

Even if you believe that voting is more than a selection of meaningless choices designed to mask the true lack of agency we have, there is a tremendous amount of money and power and influence on the other side of this equation. So don't just vote or petition to the extent that we're "from the internet," we only have a certain amount of power of our own that we can leverage within this domain. It is possible to develop user-friendly technical solutions that would stymie this type of surveillance.

Chapter 10: The USA Freedom Act

The USA Freedom Act was sold to the American public as a response to Snowden's disclosure of multiple US surveillance programs. The bill was supposed to end the NSA's bulk collection of American's domestic calling records under section 215 of the Patriot Act, and replace it with a new program that keeps the bulk data with the phone companies.

Additionally, the NSA would then need a warrant to obtain access to this data with the telcos. Exposed by Snowden's leaks, the so-called 215 program derived from part of NSA's Stellarwind Program (STLW). On the morning of the deciding vote for the USA Freedom Act an article ran in the Wall Street Journal in which Michael V. Hayden, former director of the CIA, referred to the USA Freedom Act as "NSA Reform that only ISIS could love".

In spite of that statement, after the USA Freedom Act became law, Hayden admitted that the net effect of the new law was trivial. In an on-stage interview at a Wall Street Journal conference two weeks after the act was passed Hayden said:

"If somebody would come up to me and say 'Look, Hayden, here's the thing: this Snowden thing is going to be a nightmare for you guys for about two years. And then when you get all done with it, what you're going to be required to do is that little 215 program about American telephony metadata and by the way, you can still have access to it, but you got to go to court and get access to it from the companies, rather than keep it yourself", I go, 'And this is it after two years? Cool'."

In making this point, Hayden pinched his fingers together to emphasize how tiny the effects of the legislative changes had been to the data collection program.

It should be noted, if you review the data preservation policy of any of the major telecom carriers, they now keep all their Call Detail Records (CDR) effectively forever. Phone companies use this same "metadata" for their own analytics. It is, for example, how they decide where to put in new cell towers, or where they need to install new switches for additional capacity. Before, the NSA kept their own copy of this data, and although I'm not convinced they still don't, consider the following: as the bulk of the NSA budget (that we can see) is already doled out to 3rd party contractors, why wouldn't they do so in this case? This same data is bought and sold every day in the private sector. It would be seriously naive for any American to think the NSA doesn't have a business relationship with any one of the hundreds of companies that buy the metadata from the telcos. But the NSA doesn't need to actually buy the data from these data analysis companies, why bother?

The NSA gives these firms the algorithms they want run, their shopping list, and the companies run the queries. Then the NSA gets back a full color report on any targeting data they so desire. With the pretty report in hand, they can go to a federal judge for an instant warrant to tidy up the legal end of things, if even needed. And as we have discussed, to date, not a single federal judge as ever asked to see the SQL code or algorithm that came up with any pretty reports.

If you want to get into the big data business yourself, feel free to call up Verizon's "Precision Market Insights" division, as that's the group that actually sells Verizon's cellular customer's geolocational data. They will be happy to tell you that they don't actually include the account name with the cellular ID numbers. They will quote you the success that professional sports franchises have had with their product, and how they use it to track the cell phones of people that attend their sporting events to see what businesses they go to after the game, or where they live, so they can better spend their ad budgets. And although that's certainly true, any amateur SQL programmer can match a GPS tag to a physical address via comparative data sets. And obviously, it's not hard to get white-page like address data.

For example, if five phones "live" at your house, it's easy to figure out which is which. Some of those phones spend a lot of time at certain places of business, and some of them spend a lot of time at certain elementary or high schools. Thus a single data broker can overlay your family's entire physical location history on top of existing credit, workplace, and educational data. Big businesses use this data every day, as does the NSA, and now even large and well organized criminal organizations.

As the former CIA director pointed out, The USA Freedom Act of 2014 only made trivial changes. Big data is still doing its thing, and in the world of big data, every citizen becomes a product that's for sale.

Chapter 11: Law Enforcement & Data Analysis

Law Enforcement is currently using data analysis systems such as those offered by the company Palantir. This Silicon Valley corporation originated out of a PayPal fraud detection division before being funded by the CIA via its In-Q-Tel start-up arm. Unlike the cumbersome and complex systems of the past, the Palantir systems have a smooth and intuitive GUI that makes advanced data analysis as easy as a McDonald's Point-of-Sale system. Their commercial systems are constantly improved and refined, allowing law enforcement to tie together disparate databases for comparative analysis. This technology allows your average Law Enforcement Officer (LEO) to quickly tie together multiple databases and generate beautiful full color reports that can be quite convincing when presented to a judge for a warrant.

To date, we have it on good authority that a judge hasn't asked to see the actual algorithm that generated the reports, but that's another topic for another time. What's important is that a system like this will allow a LEO to generate a report of everyone that has a phone that hangs out with a phone of a known drug dealer, and also has a large number of cash deposits at his bank. At first glance that seems like a great idea. All a cop has to do is push a button and he can instantly identify the money behind any drug operation, right? So it is a good idea, in theory. In practice, if you happen to be someone that owns a car wash, that also happens to regularly have breakfast at the same Starbucks as a known drug dealer, then that's an issue.

An intrinsic problem with big data is that it's too much for one human to get their head around. This creates a special set of problems when you put someone with a myopic worldview in front of a powerful data analysis system, especially Law Enforcement. Obviously if each LEO had a background in computer science, SQL, and a full understanding of advanced mathematics, it wouldn't be a problem. Of course if they had that level of education, they wouldn't be working in Law Enforcement for well under $70K a year. The psychology of confirmation bias causes erroneous arrests every day as it is, but with these powerful new tools a LEO can now thoroughly convince himself, and others, of even the most obscure "criminal" connections. This is often done with complete disregard for any other logical explanation. But these systems aren't built to find alternative and logical explanations, they are simply made to compare data points. This is a perfect storm scenario for confirmation bias.

One could remark that it's odd that those enforcing the law aren't required to have a law degree, or even to know 10% of the law. That shouldn't matter with a functional judicial system, but that side of things is broken as well. In the United States over 90% of cases are decided by plea agreements. When a citizen is faced with a possibility of a 20 year sentence for going to trial, as opposed to a guarantee of only 5 years for taking a plea, it's just a pragmatic decision to accept the plea. With that in mind, it's even more concerning that people are being targeted for criminal activities by Law Enforcement Officers with plug-and-play systems that they have little understanding of. There is no oversight, no accountability, and no democratic process whatsoever involved in the creation or choice of algorithms used in Law Enforcement targeting.

So what we are left with is depending on the corporate programmers to write perfect code. However, those coders answer to their employers, whose goal is not perfect justice, but the increased sales of the analysis systems. To sell analysis systems, those systems have to find people when Law Enforcement pushes the target button, and so they make sure they do.

Factoring in the fact that Law Enforcement agencies have already been found to be engaged in for-profit seizure operations, the obvious next step is that these systems are also targeting people for arrest based on their financial data.

Chapter 12: The Foreign Compliance Tax Act (FACTA)

The US continues its public war on wealth in efforts to ensure the peasant vote. Combined with economic policy that creates a never ending supply of peasants, this has been a tried and true strategy for the US government. Peasants are certainly easier to govern than millionaires. When the government does something stupid and entirely self-serving against the will of the people, the wealthy tend to just give the government the finger and sail off on their yachts. The problem for the government in this scenario is that the wealthy tend to take their money with them when they go. Meanwhile, the peasants suffer the bad government policy, and the loss of jobs when the captains of industry leave.

As the US has continued to turn the population against business owners, investors, and captains of industry, they had no problem getting the Foreign Compliance Tax Act (FACTA) passed in late 2010. Tax law is boring and tedious by design. No one but Chief Financial Officers and Accountants really ever have to read it. As words on paper go, the FACTA isn't very threatening. But like all acts, laws, policy, and regulations, it's just the legal excuse for a nation-state to take an individual's money when that person fails to perfectly adhere to all the fine print in the country's voluminous laws. With that in mind, the FACTA is actually the grim reaper to the personal preservation of wealth.

Due to their new arduous and punishing tax laws, more US citizens are renouncing their citizenship, and more Offshore Financial Centers (OFC) are refusing to provide private banking services to US citizens. At this point in history there is very little reason to maintain citizenship in a debt ridden country with an irresponsible, warmongering government. Although once you leave the US you do run the risk of becoming a victim of its disastrous foreign policy, but that's a topic for another time. What's important here is understanding that FACTA is the legal premise under which the US government can force offshore banks to report every detail of any US citizen's banking. These banks that participate in FACTA have to report any US account holder with over $10,000 in their account to the US Internal Revenue Service (IRS). In this case the word "internal" is used rather loosely. Banks can face steep penalties for failing to report US citizens, thus many banks choose to simply deny services to Americans.

There are over 190 countries on the planet, and only one requires mountains of paperwork to bank with, so this is an easy decision for foreign banks. None of which is fair to the other countries, because the US is the biggest offshore tax haven for everyone on the planet but US citizens. Controlling the default banking currency apparently has its privileges, but that monopoly can't last.

In one fell swoop the US government eliminated the vast majority of possibilities for US citizens to move their wealth abroad. No longer can a US citizen just walk into a foreign bank and open an account with any expectations of privacy and security. That being said, with the current state of intelligence agency involvement in international finance, opening an account in a personal name was a dumb idea to begin with. Even if the banks didn't willingly comply, the US Central Intelligence Agency (CIA) is going to pay a bank employee to leak the customer data, as they have in the past, repeatedly.

So in spite of FACTA, corporate accounts continue to function as asset protection tool when setup correctly. Personal ownership of anything of real value is no longer viable. Aircraft, boats, and anything but your primary residence (if in the US) can be exposed to civil litigation. Concerning the governments, they can and will take your home even though most US state law shields the primary residence from civil seizure. It's just too easy to go corporate to justify not doing so. In the case of FACTA there is no other way to protect your wealth effectively, and so an offshore corporation becomes essential.

Chapter 13: CryptoCurrency for n00bs

Chances are, you have heard of Bitcoin, as most people in the first world have by now. Even if you are completely new (a n00b) to the online world, Bitcoin makes the news quite often. You may have even used Bitcoin, but I find that there is a very small percentage of people that understand how it works. I've read all the white-papers (a technical document on the inner workings of any particular technology), I have viewed the source code for Bitcoin, and I have played with the code. I can truly appreciate the work that went into the project, and its implications for the future. The conceptual model is truly a work of art, even if it has a few flaws with data size. I wish everyone could appreciate cryptocurrency as much as I do, but for some reason not everyone has a background in advanced mathematics, cryptography, and computer science. I blame public schools.

In my efforts to explain basic cryptography I failed to find a suitable one-stop-shop I could send my associates to for a comprehensive and easy to understand explanation. Over time, I have repeatedly simplified my cryptography explanation until I arrived at the below explanation. This is as simple as it gets. Beyond this we'd have to get out an abacus and fully devolve. From this point we must proceed with the understanding that my dear reader knows basic multiplication, and has played Scrabble or Words with Friends at least once in their life.

In the game of Scrabble you get 7 tiles with letters on them, or a blank for a wild card, and you have to try to make words with them to play on the board. For this explanation, there will be no blanks, and we don't even need the board. Let's assume that any combination of letters can be a "word", and that we don't even have the full 7 tiles. Let's say you have only two, and A and a B. With those you have two "characters" and two "positions"; a positions being a spot on the rack for a character, and in this example we are assuming only two spots.

With these limitations, you can make only two words: AB, and BA. That's it. But if you had an unlimited number of A's, and B's, but were still confined to only two positions, you could then make: AA, AB, BA, and BB.

Mathematically, the formula (henceforth referred to as an algorithm) is [Number of possible characters] to the power of the [Number of possible positions]. So in this case 2 squared, (which is 2 multiplied by itself 1 time) equals 4 possible words.

If we had a big bag of tiles with the letter C to use as well, we could spell AA, AB, BA, BB, AC, CA, BC, CB, and CC. Which is 9 possible words, which is the result of the same algorithm with a 3 (the number of characters) to the power of 2 (the number of positions). And so the math is 3 squared (3 times 3).

With this algorithm in mind, we can quickly calculate the maximum possible words for the A, B, and C tiles, with 3 allowed positions, as this is 3 to the third power, which is 3 times 3 times 3, or 3 multiplied by itself 3 times. This is referred to as 3 to the third power, or 3 cubed. Thus the total is 27.

If we had all 26 letters to use, and we had the full 7 positions at our disposal, the total is a factor of magnitude higher. This would be 26 to the seventh power, a total of 8,031,810,176 possible words. That's with the assumption that we are only using the uppercase of each letter. If we were to use the upper and lower case of each letter, it would mean the number of possible word combinations was 52 to the seventh power, which is (1.028071703×10 to the 12th power). Which is a very large number, well in excess of your expected odds of winning any lottery. If we add a single extra position, the number jumps by another factor of magnitude to (5.345972853×10 to the 13th power).

This is why we always want the highest number of characters and positions allowed in a password, as it creates the highest number of possibilities, and reduces the likelihood of a successful guess by brute force.

Assuming you can use upper and lower case letters and numbers, then you are working with 62 characters. Even a 9 position password would be hard to guess with brute force. In reality, most applications allow you to use all 256 keyboard characters, and as many as 16 positions, which is (3.402823669×10 to the 38th power),. Even with massive computing power, that's a hard password to guess via brute force, which is why random characters are always better than names that can be attacked with a dictionary attack, but more on that later. That's enough math for now, we'll come back to the math in a moment. The take away here is that this algorithm makes really big combinations, and it's hard to brute force or guess.

To understand Bitcoin or any similar cryptocurrency, you need to understand the blockchain. The cryptography that makes Bitcoin work is a fairly complex piece of code, but if you take out the crypto piece, the blockchain is simply an accounting ledger. Assuming you remember paper checkbook registers, or you've used Quickbooks, or online banking, then you've seen an accounting register. Generally speaking, these function in line with Generally Accepted Accounting Principles (GAP), which is to simply say double-entry bookkeeping.

Without going to deep into the details of accounting, here's an example in a simple spreadsheet representing a customer's personal account view, followed by the black hat vendors account view:

Account#1 (Customer's Personal Account):

Transaction ID	Date	Memo	Debits	Credits	Balance
1000	5/20	a black hat	19.95	0.00	-19.95

Account#2 (Vendor's Business Account):

Transaction ID	Date	Memo	Debits	Credits	Balance
2000	5/20	a black hat	0.00	19.95	+19.95

The above represent what it might look like in the BitCoin wallets of the customer and vendor in a transaction involving the sale of a black hat. Although generally you couldn't buy anything if you had a negative balance, so the above is just to represent the fact that the customer spent $19.95, and the vendor received $19.95. What really matters is the master ledger, which is ultimately what the blockchain is, which would appear as follows:

The Blockchain View:

Transaction ID	Date	Memo	Debit Account	Credit Account	Amount
3000	5/20	a black hat	1000	2000	19.95

In reality, each account will have its own transaction ID, and then one shared with the master ledger, as each account is simply a snapshot of the blockchain in which their own transactions appear. Without getting into the technical specifications of the Blockchain, for our purposes here, it's just an accounting ledger as seen in the above examples.

Every Bitcoin transaction that has ever occurred is documented in this master ledger, and it does so via an algorithm that builds on the previous transactions. For explanation purposes, we'll refer to this master ledger as simply the blockchain from this point. We all share access to this blockchain. Everyone can see every transaction. To be clear, every transaction is 100% visible to the public. Bitcoin is only anonymous if you make it anonymous, which we'll get to in a moment. Fortunately the blockchain doesn't use "Account 101" or "Account 102". Instead the blockchain uses large strings of pseudo-random characters a factor of magnitude higher than anything you could get on a Scrabble rack. The number combinations possible is so large that's it's far less likely for you to be able to guess any particular private key (the account number) than it would be for you to win the lottery, twice, while being struck by lightning, twice.

The way the transactions work is a public/ private key system. Your private key generates a public key. The public key is used to encode data that can only be decoded with your private key. You and only you have access to your private key, and it's safe to give the public key to anyone that wants to send you money. All the keys are stored in the blockchain. It's possible for someone to link all your transactions on the blockchain together, but to prevent that you merely need to use a one-time use "child key". This is a feature in most Bitcoin wallet applications, which is what you'd usually use to access the Bitcoin system, and to participate on the blockchain.

Your private key is used to generate a child key, which is used to generate a new public key, which can still be decrypted with the main private key, via the child key. This prevents your transactions from being tied together. This is a feature in Bitcoin, and LiteCoin.

To summarize, cryptocurrency is a technology that utilizes a shared but encrypted accounting ledger. It's astronomically improbable to computationally brute force this technology in any way. At its core, the technology is secure beyond even the resources of the US NSA's capability to crack. That being said, every black hat knows you don't attack a bank through the front door. So we must examine the bigger picture.

Before getting into the details of Bitcoin, please note that there are services that offer to "tumble" your BitCoins. These are effectively laundering services. If you want to pay $1,000 to Bill to buy carnivorous plant seeds in a state that has banned those, you can pay a small fee to use a tumble service. You pay them in one transaction of $1,000, and then randomly allocate the money to different accounts, and then back out of those accounts, maybe in dozens of random transactions, and then back out to Bill's account. Although other security professionals recommend using these services, I would have to suspect that the US FBI might be running a few of these services just to get in the middle of the transactions to see whose buying and selling what.

My advice is to operate a large number of Bitcoin accounts, and routinely move money in and out of the accounts yourself. You might even automate that process. There's no penalty as Bitcoin has no transaction fees. Then before making a purchase, pool up the minimum funds in one account, generate a child key, and then use the tumbling service or just complete the transaction directly. Keep up with the number of accounts you have, and retire them regularly, and create new ones, only linking them together through child keys.

Chapter 14: BitCoin & LiteCoin

BitCoin is fat. As it carries around every encrypted transaction in its blockchain, and adds more transactions every minute, it's putting on a lot of extra weight. This weight is stored in gigabytes. Most smart phones lack the resources to store the full blockchain. Different "wallets" and "BitCoin Clients" (the software and/or applications used for your side of the technology) deal with the extra weight in different ways. Some do everything in the cloud, so you don't actually have your own private key on your device, or there's a copy elsewhere. Some black hats have setup fake wallet and BitCoin software just to get people to sign up and buy BitCoin for them to steal. Not cool.

For explanation purposes, a BitCoin is merely the increment in which the transactions are logged into the blockchain, which have an exchange rate against the US Dollar, Euro, Yen, Yuan, and etc. You do not have to spend an even BitCoin to use BitCoin as the blockchain is perfectly able to use the decimal system to make change.

The only way to be 100% sure you are using BitCoin securely is to run the full client, and endure the extremely slow process of your machine downloading the full blockchain to get started, and then again when you update it. The full stand-alone client is available from the BitCoin site itself. My advice is to only use that software. The process will be a bit tedious, but it's a near foolproof solution. If it was my BitCoin account, I'd install to the full BitCoin client software on a remote server in a Tier-1 datacenter with plenty of bandwidth, instead of trying to juggle that bandwidth weight via a DSL or cable modem. However, if you have the patience and the bandwidth it is possible to do. Personally, I'd go with an encrypted partition setup with VeraCrypt on a Linux machine too, but more on that later.

An alternative to the rather fat BitCoin is LiteCoin, which is as the name implies, is a lighter weight. Its whole design is made with that process in mind. As an analogy, LiteCoin is usually referred to as being the silver to BitCoin's gold. It's better suited for higher transaction volume, and lower dollar amounts. I suggest using a combination of the two technologies, with multiple accounts of each.

To get money into BitCoin or LiteCoin you need to either buy them locally via cash, or use a Virtual Currency Exchange. The exchanges allow you to transfer money from bank accounts via ACH or SWIFT (wire transfer) to the exchange, to purchase BitCoin. Some allow you to convert in and out of PayPal as well, although they are in violation of PayPal's Acceptable Use Policy (AUP) in doing so. Although some reputable exchanges do it, they are in a constant battle with PayPal's Risk Management division to make those services available. Furthermore, there have been some very high profile failures of Virtual Currency Exchanges in the past. One called MtGox collapsed after a hacking incident, taking over $300 Million with it. Use these services with caution as a convenience, but I don't suggest using them for big money. The safest way to buy BitCoin is to trade goods or cash for it.

This next technique is a little low-tech, especially for my tastes. I am truly not a people person, in spite of the FBI and media's proclamations as to my con man skills. Nevertheless, there is such a thing as "BitCoin Local". This is a scene, supported by various apps, similar to Tinder, but to buy BitCoin from strangers instead of just having sex with them. Like Craigslist, or any other "meet a stranger" app, don't do dark alleys or bad neighborhoods. Otherwise it's perfectly possible to find, for example "Joe: I have BitCoin for $400, minimum purchase $800, maximum $4,000" and see Joe's customer rating, just like on eBay. Then you can meet Joe at the mall, give him the money, and your public key (expressed as a graphic Q-Code on your smart phone), and then verify you have the coins in your wallet. The process only takes a few minutes.

I'm not a huge fan of BitCoin Local, but from an OpSec perspective it certainly reduces your digital footprint. The process works in reverse too if you need to sell BitCoin for cash. This is a good way to get started in BitCoin, at which point you can then buy and sell goods and services on the dark web. A word to the wise, use your own choice of BitCoin Wallet Software (Apps), and the full blockchain. If a stranger tells you to use a special version, chances are it's a scam. And only use apps from the BitCoin site, iTunes, or Google Play. Do not use anything from anywhere else unless it's Open Source, and you know and trust the source.

Another option to acquire BitCoin is the BitCoin ATM. These aren't on every corner, so you'll have to search for the one nearest you. In my experience ATMs tend to have cameras, and again, if I was the FBI I'd certainly deploy BitCoin ATMs with cameras and follow up on anyone with high deposits or withdrawals. In fact, I'd link that data directly back to the FBI Case Management System. I just don't trust the police state to pass up an opportunity to gather free intel, but these BitCoin ATMs may be perfectly safe outside the US. And of course, you can always wear a disguise. Thus concludes the obligatory mainstream ways to buy BitCoin.

As a black hat, and one that rather loathes mass surveillance, I have a few other ideas. In the past we've run successful scams leasing business equipment with perfectly fake corporate credit, and then selling the gear on eBay. It may sound petty, but done right it yields a couple million in profit in under 6 months, long before anyone calls the FBI. In running such an operation it was critical to look at eBay and determine what business equipment was selling in the highest volumes at the closest to the retail price. As a lot of businesses have a lot of money in PayPal to begin with, we often got 99% of the retail price when we picked wisely on items such as Cisco Switches, or desktop computers. We'd lease what we knew we could sell fast for the most money, but always very common business equipment, and never the high fraud items like laptops. The key here is the mainstream, and the most average items.

Now back to the BitCoin universe, where a similar technique can be executed. If you cruise the dark web or just the gray areas of the deep web, there is no shortage of things you can buy with BitCoin. Some main stream vendors even allow payment in BitCoin, as well as PayPal, and Credit Cards. In this case, it's simply a matter of making a short spreadsheet of what you can acquire by any means necessary, and then resell for BitCoin at the closest price to what you paid.

For example, you can use PayPal, prepaid giftcards, or cash to buy gear that you can sell for BitCoin. Once you accept the payment to one of your child keys, you can move the money around through multiple BitCoin accounts, in effect tumbling the transactions yourself. Then drop the accounts in the middle of the process every so often.

If you are super paranoid, only use your accounts once, then take all but a few dollars back out of them, and then post the keys online for some random person to use. Nothing screws up the process of vectoring a target like bad data. Which is why black hats always post their giftcard numbers online after using them to lease servers and such. I used to post mine in n00b comments on hacker forums like "How can I tell if this Credit Card Number is good 4237

", and then letting the users have their fun.

Obviously any transaction online leaves a digital trail, but the merchandise that comes in and goes back out under different names, accounts, and zip codes, is pretty obscure. If Bob pays Mary $100 that's a single line in a database. However, back to Scrabble math, if Bob has a dozen accounts, and Mary has a dozen account, and Bob breaks up the $100 and moves it in and out of him own accounts before trickling it over to Mary's accounts, which she then moves in and out of her own accounts, then that transaction becomes computationally unfeasible to reconstruct. This is the point of the tumbling service, and any of those outside the US may be fine to use, but if you can do it yourself, then that's as solid as it gets.

Here's why it matters. If you buy $100 worth of illicit drugs per month in BitCoin from the dark web, and you use the same public key, the US Drug Enforcement Agency (DEA) can later reassemble every transaction and charge you with the full weight of the total purchases. And they do this every day with regular banking transactions. Transactions that have been fully tumbled with multiple single-use disposable one-time child keys can't be reconstructed. Even if you were to only use a few keys, at least you'd have some plausible deniability.

Summary: BitCoin and LiteCoin can be used safely and anonymously, but only when using child keys, multiple accounts, and tumbling. Look for apps with these features built-in if you have to, but try to find ones that use the full blockchain as well.

Other newer crypto currencies address these issues in various ways, and offer support for multi-sig as well. Compare and contrast each to find the one that meets your needs, but as of early 2018 Ethereum, Dash, and Ripple were leading the pack behind BitCoin and LiteCoin. Check the CoinBase website to make sure whichever one you are using as a significant user base with adequate capitalization to be around awhile. Cryptocurrencies come and go, but rarely do they do so overnight. With total capitalization in the hundreds of billions of dollars, there are now thousands of businesses with websites reporting on every aspect of the markets.

Chapter 15: Targeting Algorithms

As discussed in previous chapters, law enforcement agencies use a variety of data sources to target people for investigations that can lead to seizures. The citizen sheep might actually complain if NSA was discovered to have a whole department setup with the express purpose to evaluate, rate, and monitor the status of US citizens with an eye for seizure potential. They have no such department, because they don't need one. There are many private companies that have been established by former government operatives for the sole purpose of serving the government's ongoing interests in data collection and analytics.

Although it's not generally acceptable for the government to keep track of someone's credit worthiness, no one complains when a private company does it. These pseudo-government agencies often have slick websites regarding "credit risk assessment" based on "proprietary algorithmic analysis" with no mention of the fact that their only customers are government agencies. Ostensibly these exist as an extension of US intelligence agencies to prevent terrorism. Americans have traded their most precious civil liberties and privacy for security.

As long as the government can listen to every phone call, read every text or email, and see every single financial transaction, you can be one one-hundredth of a half of a percent safer from an astronomically improbable terrorist attack. That's a good deal, right? I mean, when an Afghani refugee from Europe decides to strike back at America for their drone strike on his little sister's wedding, you'll be glad the NSA can intercept his PayPal transactions.

For your information, explosives are made from nitrogen. Most of the air you are breathing right now, is nitrogen, not oxygen. It's a trivial process to obtain nitrogen from air, and basic chemistry to convert that to explosives. Any idiot could do it, and it's not even especially dangerous, nor does it require a lot of complex equipment. It's something I was doing myself 30 years ago in my garage, long before I was 16 years old. So what exactly is it that big data can save you from? Old chemistry books? Feed store purchases made in cash? Did you know that the prime source for Ammonium Nitrate, which is what was used in the Oklahoma City bombing, is actually chicken poop? And how exactly does giving up all your civil rights to the NSA help them track the digestive movements of a billion chickens?

These algorithms do damn little to protect anyone from terrorism, as they weren't designed to. A few years ago the ACLU submitted a Freedom of Information Act (FoIA) request to the DEA regarding their Automatic Plate Recognition System deployments. They mistakenly replied to it honestly, without redaction. These systems read and catalog all the traffic passing a certain point on the highway, and match them to cell phone data, and with multiple data collection points you can match a phone to a car, and vice versa. In the DEA's FoIA reply, the purpose of this program was spelled out as "for profit" via targeted seizures. Public safety didn't even get an honorable mention.

It is real simple people, mass surveillance isn't about protection, it's about control. To believe anything else is simply willful blindness. Terrorists simply pay cash, steal, or buy things in person, because they know how the police state works. They are operators too, and they do what it takes not to get caught. If there was really a billion Muslims out to get America then things would be blowing up all day every day. As easy as it is, I am constantly surprised that there aren't dozens of politically motivated bombings everyday especially by gauging the mainstream media's level of rhetoric.

And that's the point, it's an awful lot of hype, when in reality there are damn few real people willing to throw their lives away for any cause, much less to impair America with a slight blemish that won't live for three days in the news cycle. So the entire infrastructure of the police state apparatus remains to control the civilian population. Why in the hell does the FBI need credit records? When in the history of mankind has a terrorist taken out a loan to finance a terrorist act? And even if one did, is his FICO Score and payment history really relevant?

Regardless of the reasons, the truth is very simple. In every incident where you later find out what your dear leaders were doing 20 years after the fact, it's been the same story. The government uses whatever means is technically possible at the time to monitor as much of the population as possible. The director of the NSA was once quoted as saying: "Our job is to collect it all... ", leaving the law and disclosure to others. Thus as a black hat, we assume our OpFor is always just behind the bleeding edge of technology. You should do the same where your money is concerned. Assume the worst, and plan accordingly.

It doesn't matter if the FBI really uses credit inquiries in their algorithms. Assume they do. Does your bank sell their denied loan applications to lower tier lenders where it could land in the hands of hackers? Yes, of course they do. Does the state motor vehicle registry feed data to the FBI? For certain. Do insurance companies sell data to the feds about who's on the insurance for which luxury car? Yes, they do. And accordingly, if you are using an offshore holding company for a high end car, it can still be tied to you if the insurance is in your name. If the credit and tax filings don't appear to indicate that you can afford that particular car, then that is a vector within a database that can lead to problems.

Big data analytics is a diverse and growing industry with extensive government collusion. It's no place for optimism regarding the fine print in privacy policies. To protect yourself you have to assume your OpFor has access to anything and everything you have ever put online, or on paper that could later be entered by some data entry type, or Optical Character Recognition (OCR) system. That's the tech used to scan paper documents into paperless filing systems. If you go ahead and make those assumptions, you can save yourself a lot of grief in the future. The specifics of how the algorithms work isn't important to protect your personal wealth. Err in favor of caution. Assume your OpFor has it all, and can compare it all. If that's the standard you set for your OpSec, you can't go wrong.

Chapter 16: Wealth & Success

This book is intended to be a crash course in "Offshore Banking, Asset Protection, and Understanding Financial Surveillance Systems". This is a no-holds-barred approach without the political correctness or national bias usually found anywhere financial advice is offered. This book was designed for those of you that have recently come into wealth, or for those that intend to do so successfully. For many people, they will come to the quite logical conclusion that being wealthy simply isn't worth the effort, especially after reading the first few chapters of this book. That is understandable. However, for those of you that are determined to gain and sustain true wealth, and to build a solid foundation for your luxurious lifestyle, then all the information you need to do so is now in your hands. Once you learn the rules of the game, and how the system works, you can begin mastering the art of gaming the system.

The purpose of this book is not to illuminate a path to wealth, or to promote one venture or investment strategy versus another. The point of this book is to assist those lucky enough to achieve a high level of wealth in the extremely difficult task of keeping their wealth. It's important to understand that once you make money, it doesn't magically become immune to the rest of the economy, not even if it's hidden under your mattress. No matter where you keep your money, there will always be a number of people, organizations, and governments that will be working very diligently to take your money.

If you think you haven't made enough money to worry about needing creative banking solutions, consider this: how can you ever hope to accumulate wealth if you can't hang on to it?

Unlike many books, websites, and advisors that promote a few loopholes in the system, from this book you will learn not just a variety of current tried-and-true methods, but the techniques to find and exploit new holes in the system. Many books stop short of offending the position of their government, or current political administrations. These books claim to offer comprehensive information, and yet they avoid advising the reader on tactics to avoid the biggest threat to wealth out there: governments. Here, a different approach is taken.

You will not be advised on what is or is not illegal, only what works and what does not. As this book is written for international readership, it would not be fair to avoid educating the readers in Mexico. For example, even Mexico doesn't require their offshore citizens to return taxes back to their home country, merely because the US does.

The United States has the strictest laws in the developed world, as well as the harshest collection practices, so the US will be used as an example of one extreme or another throughout this book. US law fills entire libraries, and in an effort to keep this book portable, those laws won't be included here. In cases where it would be prudent to pay attention to the potential for obvious violations of US law, it will be mentioned.

There are over 190 countries on Planet Earth, and the United States is only one of them. It may come as a shock to United States citizens, but the US no longer leads in healthcare, technology, education, or anything meaningful to humanity as a whole. What the US does lead in is debt, crime, drug use, and taxes. The US currently has the highest corporate tax rate in the world. As the US battles their internal political problems facing one debt crisis after another, it will continue to be an environment that is very hostile to wealth. Specific information will be provided accordingly to assist US readers, and those that intend to do business in the US. This book does not attempt to provide legal advice in line with the United States' ever changing laws. If you need legal advice hire a lawyer. If you need to build a system to secure your wealth from all opposing forces, read on.

What is wealth? When many people think of success, happiness, power, and their ultimate life goals, wealth is always at the top of the list, and rightfully so. You can't very well advance in life without being able to afford to pay for the necessities of life, and all the icons of wealth such as exotic cars, aircraft, and yachts are not available to those without the means to pay for them. Popular Western media continues to promote these ideas as well by associating success with luxury items. Society as a whole dangles the carrot of wealth in front of us all, driving those of us with means to college, and often those of us without means to crime. At this point in human history almost every possible scheme, scam, or business venture has been tried to produce wealth. We can continue to expect people with less to try to obtain more; it's just human nature. But what is success?

One icon of success is often the private jet. It's certainly more pleasant to think of a private jet in terms of being an icon of financial achievement, versus a gaping wound on your financial portfolio that bleeds cash. The truth is that if you were given a brand new Gulfstream tomorrow it's going to depreciate in value hundreds of thousands of dollars per year, while costing you tens of thousands of dollars in maintenance, certifications, inspections, fuel, and that's not to mention what has to be paid for someone to actually fly it. Then you of course have to house it somewhere, where you must consider the insurance and taxes as well. The truth is that the more money you have the more hands come out to take it away from you. The more expensive any one item is, the more expensive it often is to keep it. That's a dirty secret of wealth, one that is often punishing to those that come into money without an education in finance. It is no secret that 9-out-of-10 lottery winners end up flat broke in less than ten years.

Throughout this book the focus will be placed firmly on using modern banking techniques to avoid hostile governments and litigants. The study of these techniques is referred to as Asset Protection. This term has many connotations. Many lawyers will sell you an asset protection plan that merely increases your odds of being able to better your position in a divorce, albeit only slightly. At the other extreme of Asset Protection one could visualize a cargo container full of vacuum sealed currency buried in the jungles of Columbia. Regardless which method would be more appropriate for which situation, within the text of this book we use the term generally to cover the full spectrum of the subject matter.

Within the scope of this book we'll fully explore virtual currencies, account opening procedures, introduction services, and all aspects of utilizing technology and non-banking services to control the flow and security of your wealth. However, it is not the intent of this book to be a "Dummy's Guide to Money Laundering". Although there is undoubtedly at least one US Attorney that would refer to this book in that light, that can't be helped. The US government often refers to any technique that reduces US tax exposure as "money laundering", or "tax evasion". That's understandable considering they are over 20 trillion dollars in debt with less than half their population being obligated to pay any taxes at all.

Considering the remainder of the population is living off government programs (entitlements), that's a real problem. Anyone with basic mathematical skills can see that the US economy, as of mid-2017, is in serious peril. This book's been compiled for the internationally minded businessman (or woman) that has a desire to keep the full proceeds of their hard work, and no desire to support failed governments or the poor. If you do want to donate to the good of humanity, you might consider a gift to an orphanage in the third-world. Chances are you will see the results of your donation there very quickly. If you sent the US government a billion dollars you can rest assured that they would waste it. It's what big governments do.

Chapter 17: Dirty Laundry

Concerning the term "money laundering", for the purposes of this book the term will refer to the actual act of moving street-level cash into the banking system. As this subject is beyond the scope of this book, it will not be discussed here in detail. There are very few businesses left that would produce cash that needs to be "laundered" that are not illegal in almost all countries (i.e. street level drug dealers, etc.). At this point in human history large governments are spending billions of dollars on law enforcement and judicial processes specifically targeting drug dealers, especially in the US.

The math is simple: the US government is 100% corrupt when it comes to drug cases; they manufacture evidence, coerce statements, and extort testimony. They have a 97% conviction rate, and that 3% that doesn't get convicted likely cut some other deal to avoid conviction. The business model of US illegal drug sales is flawed on every level, yet it continues to attract the uneducated in vast numbers, which perpetuates the US government's ability to continue to incarcerate it's citizens at the highest rate of any country in human history. The career expectancy of a first time drug dealer is 26 months, with an average sentence of 8 years. The statistical likelihood of a felon being able to avoid a return to prison within 3 years of release is only 13%; involvement with drugs cuts that number down to a fraction. Over 99% of drug dealers and/or drug users return to prison within 2 years of being released from prison. If you think you are lucky enough to beat those odds, play the lotto. The cost of failure will be $2.00, versus 8+ years of your life.

Accordingly, the focus here will be on managing wealth created through other means that do not usually involve large cash transactions, although the proper techniques for moving cash will be covered, it should be understood that large quantities of cash simply invite law enforcement investigation and seizure, even if your money is 100% legal. Gone are the days where governments follow their own laws. If you get caught with even a small sum of cash in the

US (less than $20K in some cases), you will go to jail ostensibly only until you can explain the legitimate origin of the cash. Realistically, it won't matter, you won't get it back and you'd be lucky to get out of jail.

That being said, if you had a debit card linked to a bank

account in Hong Kong with fifty million dollars in it, you wouldn't lose that.

It's simple: cash is associated with crime and criminals in the United States. The US is pushing for a full police state where all transactions are done electronically and tracked. Failure to willingly comply with their agenda could be costly. Therefore it is essential to learn the techniques taught here to appear to play by their rules where you have to in order to get your money somewhere safely out of their reach. This is the very essence of Offshore Banking: make the money where it's best to make the money, but keep the money where it's best to keep the money, and not merely in the most convenient jurisdiction (i.e. in your home country, or where you made the money).

By learning how to best utilize the techniques taught here, you can safely create as much wealth as you desire, without the stress and fear associated with the egregious practices of hostile governments, litigants, hackers, and corporations alike.

Chapter 18: Brick and Mortar Banking

There are many ways to store money and to utilize your stored money for purchases, and this process is most often referred to as banking. Ironically, banking doesn't always require a bank, and some alternatives will be discussed in later chapters. Before those alternatives can be understood, along with the pros and cons of these alternatives, one must understand conventional banking and where privacy fails. In many countries, the governments do not believe that citizens have any right to keep their financial transactions secret from said governments or taxing authorities. One could easily point out a direct correlation between countries with a lack of financial privacy and the amount of sovereign debt that those countries have, but fiscal responsibility is beyond the scope of this book and apparently the combined efforts of many large governments.

At the time of this writing in mid-2017, the European Union is not in the best of shape; Ireland and Portugal have already defaulted, and Greece is limping back. Spain and Italy are both still in bad shape as well, and if any of those large countries fail, they could take the Euro down with them. As bad off as the EU is, the combined debt of all European countries is easily eclipsed by the over $20 trillion dollar US debt.

These countries will likely fail, and fail badly, but until that time, special attention must be paid when banking in these countries. Law enforcement has forced banks to document suspicious transactions, and report them, so that the governments will have the opportunity to seize the money if they can manipulate a legal means to do so. In later chapters, what is and is not a suspicious transaction will be detailed.

Meanwhile, it must be noted that for the purposes of this book, a "bank account" is a regular corporate checking account with a regular bank, such as Chase, Wells Fargo, Bank of America, etc. There are almost no useful purposes for a personal checking account, and small business accounts are totally useless for the smooth transfer of large sums of money to safe and secure domiciles: the ultimate goal.

When a bank account is opened in a country like the US, the bank will require "Corporate Docs" and in almost all cases, some form of identification. In the US two forms of ID are usually required. However, this process can be manipulated by opening accounts onine, or by using a "fake ID". Please not that there is a huge difference

Between using identification that portrays a fictional person, versus using identification that assumes the identity of a real person without their permission. That can be the difference between a state misdemeanor and a federal felony. Identity theft is not necessary, or advised, for financial privacy.

When you open a US bank account with a state issued driver's license, the bank does not have the ability to check that 10 against a state database. The bank only checks the ID against TeleCheck, CheckRight, or any number of hot check databases. Other than that, the ID is only used for internal bank records, it is saved to a file, and stored. This information is not shared with the federal government (yet) unless it is subpoenaed during a legal process. Otherwise, should you find it advantageous to do so, you could open a bank account with authentic looking fake state ID.

On the other side of the desk at the bank will be a business banker. This individual would like to open an account for you, as that brings his bank more business. This individual works for a profit hungry corporation, not the federal government. As with any business deal, it is important to understand the goals and motivations of all involved. Assuming you are not dressed like you are there to rob the place, and you speak educated English, the business banker will do everything in their power to assist you with the account opening process. However, they do have rules they have to follow.

It is almost impossible to completely avoid banks while moving around large amounts of money. Virtual currencies, precious metals, and investment grade diamonds all offer alternatives to traditional banking, but each with its own caveats. These will be discussed in later chapters. It is safe to assume that no matter what course is chosen to secure wealth, and to establish proper asset protection, some traditional banking will be required. Although anyone should be able to do something as simple as opening a corporate bank account, those that choose to pay special attention to their financial privacy will want to take the following under advisement.

The business banker will request two forms of ID, a Social Security Number for every signer, and the Employer Identification Number (EIN) for the corporation. Notice the word "request" was used, and not require. For expediency purposes the usual process involves the provision of a state issued driver's license, and a Social Security card. However, a Social Security card, or number, is not necessarily required to open a US bank account. What is required is two forms of ID, a primary, and a secondary.

The Primary ID

For a primary ID one must provide a state or government issued photo ID. This can be a passport, driver's license, state ID card, US passport card, military ID, or similar identification. Theoretically, a concealed carry permit would work as well, but as you want this stage of the process to go as smoothly as possible, a state driver's license is the best choice. Again, if this was a good fake ID, the bank would merely photocopy it and throw it in a file. In some college towns where there are a large number of college students, especially at a state university, the banks may accept a college ID as a primary ID. If you look the part, this may be an option for you. But college students don't usually move hundreds of thousands of dollars, so that fact deserves scrutiny.

The Secondary ID

For the second form of ID, the bank will accept any of the above or a Social Security card, pilot's license, or again any state or government issued ID. It's important to note, that the secondary ID does not require a photograph. In the past, banks have accepted public library cards, or even credit cards from other banks, but the technical requirements specify a state or government ID. A copy of a certified birth certificate would work, and that's just a piece of paper. A marriage license is also just a piece of paper, but it is of course issued by the state via a county office. Again, the bank can not verify the authenticity of any of the aforementioned documents.

The Social Security Number

A bank cannot require you to disclose your Social Security Number, but they will ask for it. In the days preceding 9/11 and The Patriot Act, privacy became tantamount to supporting terrorism. However, all the new regulatory hassles of the Patriot Act badly hurt the banking business. Some experts believe that the additional requirements at banks spawned the plethora of check cashing businesses and prepaid debit card markets. Either way, the once rigorously enforced policies are now often merely "best effort" attempts to get additional documentation on account holders. The Social Security Number falls into this gray area as well. Thanks to the massive number of identity theft cases, it's now "cool" to say "Sorry, I don't provide my Social Security Number". Instead of looking like a terrorist or worse yet, a Libertarian, now the statement demonstrates responsibility, caution, and prudence, exactly what a bank wants in a customer.

That being said, alternative ID will have to be provided. For a corporate bank account the EIN is used as a primary account marker; i.e. when you call the bank, that is the first thing they will ask for when filling out the corporate account forms. An X can be put in the Social Security field with the following explanation "... although I currently serve as an officer of the corporation, by corporate policy I cannot commingle my personal credit worthiness with that of the company". This makes perfect sense. A private equity company would loathe the acquisition of a company that has heavily entangled personnel. Personal guarantees and obligations are to be avoided at all costs for a real corporation, as it is taught in any MBA program. Accordingly, it no longer appears even remotely suspicious to decline to provide a Social Security Number (SSN) for a corporate account.

In consideration of the above, a SSN should never be provided, as the SSN is the one single piece of data that the bank, or any business, can actually verify. Any business can register with the IRS website and get free access to a portal that verifies a SSN with a name. It will not give a state, or date issued, it only verifies that the name matches the number. There are many inexpensive services that will provide a name match, in addition to the state and date of issue, although banks usually do not use these, they could still be a problem.

Some banks use Fraud Guardian, or other anti-fraud analytic engines, that check multiple databases and return a score for fraud probability. If the provided SSN comes back issued prior to the date of birth, then the probability is 100% for fraud. These services are more often used by online banks (like ING Bank) and virtual currency providers (like PayPal) and less by traditional banks, though that is subject to change. The simplest and safest solution is to not use disingenuous Social Security Numbers. Stick with the corporate accounts, and don't provide a SSN.

Chapter 19: Online Banking

The ability to open a bank account online appeared in the 1990s. At that time it was little more than a website link from a brick and mortar (physical) bank to the application forms for a new account. There was almost no more convenience as it wasn't possible to actually open the account online; the website merely enabled a prospective client to fill out the forms which were then pushed to an actual account representative. It was still necessary to print local copies of the new account forms and take them to the bank with proper ID. There was a brief period where fully online banks allowed full online account setup, but they were quickly attacked with fraudulent account setups.

Just as the rules began to relax for online accounts as network security caught up to the industry, 9/11 occurred. Within two years of 9/11 the US government was able to push through sweeping legislation to monitor all aspects of the financial system. The results of The Patriot Act were unanticipated by all but a handful of network security professionals. The regulations were ostensibly designed to track funding for "terror networks" and drugs dealers that were inadvertently "funding terrorism". In reality it could be argued that the US government was casting a large net in hopes of finding funding sources for their wars in the Middle East. Either way, the results were a net so full they couldn't lift it.

The process was supposed to require a Suspicious Transaction Form to be filed for all shady transactions the bank saw. However, the rules for what was and was not shady were not clear, and so newly formed government agencies were buried in mountains of paperwork generated by banks merely trying to cover their ass. This continued for years, allowing banks like Bank of America, HSBC, and Stanford Bank to assist in the laundering of hundreds of millions of dollars for organized criminals such as the Columbian and Mexican drug cartels. The method was simple: if a bank saw an obvious fraudulent transaction that they had to report, but it was a profitable deal for the bank, all they had to do was file the Suspicious Transaction Form on the transaction with a thousand more frivolous Suspicious Transaction Forms, and the actual cartel wire would be buried for years. The Patriot Act actually gave banks the ability to do more dirty business, and plausible deniability for their role in the process, as they had met their regulatory requirements.

This insanity continued through 2010 when the US government caught up to the banks and began issuing hundred million dollar fines. By that time Stanford Bank had already been shut down for other issues. HSBC and Bank of America had effectively given themselves no-interest loans for a decade dealing with the cartels. Even if they had to pay back 90% of the profits they made on those suspicious transactions, they never paid a dime back on the interest they made loaning that money back out. That is simply how banks work. After 2010, banking had changed significantly in response to these fines, and the fallout from the sub-prime mortgage crisis of 2008. Unable to continue to make high risk loans and to have the feds pick up the tab, banks have had to cut costs.

It is now possible to open a bank account online without utilizing any personnel at the bank, but it is not exactly easy. As of 2017 this is still an evolving situation with an ebb and flow between convenience and security, with cash strapped banks trying to keep costs down. Today, banks have given up on preventing fraud. They accept it, as they have no choice. That being said, they only accept so much. If a few online account opening systems make the bank $3 million in new accounts per month, but cost them $1 million in fraud, that's still a significant net profit and it's all about the money, in every instance. If they can allow accounts to be opened online cheaply and easily, without tying up a real employee, then they have to do it even if a percentage of the accounts are fraudulent. If there isn't any fraud, then they know that they have probably tightened the screws too tight and they must be losing new legitimate business as well.

There will always be a way to open a bank account online, even if your identity information isn't 100% legitimate. However, there is not one trick that will always work, and the banks can be expected to continue to evolve their online account opening process for more convenience and less fraud. As less fraud often means less financial privacy, this process deserves further exploration.

At first glance, just the concept of an online bank account seems to be the very essence of private banking. There are even a few banks that are online only, such as ING Bank and Ally. Since they have no retail-level physical building for potential customers to walk into, one would think their new account requirements would be ripe for fraud, and they once were. Now, they have collectively realized that most of their new customers come to them from other banks, and are not new to banking. Ally, ING, and even the brick-and-mortar banks allow easy online account setup for those that can verify they have another bank account elsewhere. This is an inconvenience for those wishing to open a brand new bank account, but it does mean that if one has the ability to get any bank account open anywhere, even at a troubled small town bank with poor security, then the account can easily be converted to a live account with any other bank via the online account setup process.

At this point it would be easy to point out specific holes in a particular bank's online account setup site. The problem with that is that by the time this book goes to print that hole will have been patched or otherwise negated. If not, once the book is published, the bank would no doubt feel the effects of those abusing this information, and then they'd close the hole. To be best served by this book, a decision has been made to examine in detail the process of finding holes, and where to look for them instead.

In line with the ability to traverse from an easy-to-open account to any other account, it is also possible to use a debit or credit card to do the same. For example, if you have a Bank of America debit card from your account with them, you can use it to fund a new Chase account online, thus verifying the name on the account, and allowing Chase to bump the responsibility of complete account verification to Bank of America. Theoretically, one could use a registered gift card instead of a debit card or a prepaid debit card. Either of those would require less documentation to acquire. The idea behind all of the above is to find the lowest common denominator to work up, get what is easiest to acquire, and work up from there.

In some cases banks have experimented with full online account setup, even Chase, the most conservative bank with the tightest relationship with the US government. In most cases an account can be opened completely online by simply uploading copies of the required documents. In this case a new account setup could be done with a JPEG image of a driver's license, versus an actual physical driver's license for which a dye-sublimation printer would be required to create. This technique works, but there are tighter account restrictions on these online account setups, so the red flags tend to go up faster, which can be problematic later.

An ideal solution is to make a list of all the banks that provide the required services, and then simply try all of their online setups,

109

and make a list of which one needs what to open a new account If, for example, a bank only allows $10,000 or under for a transaction volume on an online created account, one could view that as an inconvenience. Alternatively, it should mean that having access to ten or twenty of these accounts would allow someone to move a fair amount of money while building good account history and reducing scrutiny as they go. Remember, most financial hurdles can be circumvented with changes in scale and volume.

For example, a $50,000 wire may trigger a Suspicious Transaction Form, but fifty transactions of random dollar amounts between one and two thousand dollars may not. The key to successful banking relationships doesn't end or begin with how the account is opened. What matters is account history, and making sure your commercial account manager knows what to expect from your business in terms of volume, and then making sure that is exactly what they see, albeit with regular growth, and slow expansion of those parameters.

In the US there is a growing class divide, and a growing number of people stuck outside traditional banking systems. In the near future new options will be available, which will present new opportunities. It's important to evolve as needed, and not to pick favorite techniques. Try new options, even if you have a system that works. If Wells Fargo allows you to open a bank account online with only data from a Green Dot card, that's fine; if that works for you, use it. However, maybe you want to try Chase's new Sapphire prepaid card and see if that would work to open a Bank of America account, just to have that Information in case your technique ever fails. Banking security is a mercurial business so it's important to stay ahead of technology and banking policy, even if it requires some trial and error.

Chapter 20: Virtual Currencies

There is a growing number of virtual currencies, some that are used for everyday transactions like PayPal, and others that are more obscure. Some of these are US based with significant regulatory oversight, others are based in offshore domiciles specific for the associated benefits of Financial Privacy. These businesses come and go, but many like PayPal and G-Pay will likely continue to be a viable alternative to traditional banking. Newer cryptocurrencies such as Dash (formerly Dark Coin), Ethereum, and Ripple offer more options, and in some cases more anonymity.

As addressed in previous chapters, this book is not intended to be a step-by-step guide for the layman. Instead of merely highlighting a few paths that may or may not still exist by the time they are needed, this book attempts to teach the art of finding new paths through complex financial systems in order to establish high volume conduits for any number of uses. In short, the information presented here would be best viewed as a toolbox, versus a set of instructions for any particular project.

That being said, it will always be advantageous to do a quick internet search to verify the current status of any and all companies discussed here. Mergers, acquisitions, and dissolutions happen every day, but it is rare that a successful business model will ever cease to exist completely. In most cases, one business is quickly replaced with another, or their services are simply added to another company's offerings. This is a very common occurrence within the realm of virtual currencies and virtual currency exchanges.

Otherwise virtual currencies can be a valuable way of moving wealth from place to place, and to purchase virtual goods, physical goods, and services. With many virtual currencies, there is built-in security and privacy, with others like PayPal, they work much like a traditional bank account but with an increased ease of use for online usage.

Although PayPal requires most of the same identity information as a traditional bank account, they have an excellent dispute resolution and anti-fraud system. After a PayPal purchase, if there is a problem, there are many options available to resolve the dispute. With a traditional banking relationship, the bank doesn't offer their clients many remedies for bad business deals. PayPal can roll-back, or suspend the transaction, and post the funds into escrow until the dispute is resolved. With all virtual currencies there is a natural evolution; when they begin, they offer maximum convenience, and after they get beat up with fraud, they modernize their systems or go out of business. The older ones like PayPal have very robust systems that allow companies to do business with great ease.

PayPal will allow a link to a bank account in the US, and a US PayPal account has a certain policy for their account creation process. However, PayPal isn't a US company, they are based out of the country of Lichtenstein (central Europe). PayPal offers accounts in less security conscious countries with far less scrutiny. For example, in the US a PayPal account that bumps over $500 suddenly needs a link to a credit card or bank account; over $5,000 and PayPal will be asking for a SSN or an EIN. (Never provide an SSN when any other option exists).

In Mexico, a Mexican PayPal account will allow up to $2,000 before they ask for any additional data. As PayPal is attempting to ride the wave of economic growth in Latin America, they can be expected to make convenience a priority, and give security a back seat. Every country PayPal operates in has separate limits, requirements, and thresholds. All countries outside the US have less fraud, and thus the account requirements are less egregious minus Nigeria and extremely high fraud areas where PayPal won't even allow an account to be opened.

PayPal allows their clients to move money to and from a bank account via the actual PayPal account, and they allow for a credit card to be linked-in as well for over-draft of sorts. PayPal does not allow clients to buy prepaid debt/gift cards, or to convert PayPal to any other virtual currency. It is against their policy, and PayPal will terminate accounts for any associated activity. This policy could be for legitimate security concerns, to help them maintain their market position, or most likely both reasons and then some. Regardless, it makes it inconvenient for anyone using multiple virtual currencies. PayPal disallows their services to be used for "Adult Content", and a variety of items it deems questionable. Of all the virtual currencies, PayPal is the most conservative and stable, but that can leave a lot of need for other virtual currencies.

Enter the virtual currency exchanges. It would be great if there was a single website that would allow for the conversion of all virtual currencies, but such is not the case. If a business has $2,000 in PayPal, and the business decides to put that same $2,000 into BitCoin to buy something that can't be purchased via PayPal, it can be problematic, but it is possible. The problem is that PayPal would kill the account belonging to the virtual currency exchange, if they were able to link the account to this activity. PayPal security personnel merely search for virtual currency exchanges, and begin the transaction process, and kill the account they see there. Therefore any transactions in or out of PayPal are expensive, and more than a few of the virtual currency exchanges are total frauds merely offering the "too good to be true" service.

To reduce the chances of being ripped off by one of these fraud sites, the best practice is to only convert PayPal to and from regular bank accounts. In situation where it is critical to get a lot of money out of PayPal, it is possible to get a PayPal debit card and them simply buy gold to convert later, or of course one could setup a full credit card processing account and process the money out that way. For PayPal there are a variety of methods to move the money out. Worst case scenario you could setup other PayPal/eBay accounts, and buy fictitious items, thus dividing the lump sum stuck in PayPal by a factor of 20, then the money could be moved to bank accounts via ACH directly from PayPal, or via the PayPal debit card to gold, or a bank account via a friendly credit card processor. However it's done, PayPal to banking is safe, and banking to PayPal is safe any other scenario with PayPal may not be. Great caution should be taken with any virtual currency exchange that offers conversion in or out of PayPal.

When opening a virtual currency account, which is usually done with a wire transfer for all but PayPal, a new customer will have to verify that they fully understand the Acceptable Use Policy (AUP). This is usually a long and boring document that no one really reads. These usually have a check box with text next to it that says "I have read and understand the above". If there is any concerns with policy against virtual currency exchanges, this is where it would be found. If the account is already open, then it would be a good idea to search their help/support system for the word "exchange" and to find their policy on currency exchanges that way.

Beyond the above concerns, the more reputable virtual currency exchanges can be a valuable tool for separating wealth into different currencies, and legal domiciles. Remember, these won't be US based services, so just by transferring money into an offshore based virtual currency, you then have money in Luxembourg (or wherever the service is based) which is at least out of the reach of the US government, US creditors, or US litigants. Recommended for small volumes of money in multiple accounts, but not any large sum in any one account.

Prepaid Gift Cards

Prepaid gift cards are Visa/MasterCard branded cards that can be purchased with cash, without the need of a Social Security Number, or other identity information. These are not to be confused with prepaid debit cards which are reloadable and usually require additional identity information. The prepaid gift cards are never reloadable, but are usually available at check-out counters, online, or at the guest service desk of shopping malls.

Most of these can be "registered" for online usage. As a sizable chunk of the prepaid gift card market is teenagers, these issuers of prepaid gift cards usually allow for a card holder to go to a website and enter the card number, with the CVV2 code from the back of the card, and then login to an account for that card. Then it is a simple matter to enter an address, name, and phone number for the "card holder". Once that is completed, any credit card processor can verify this address in their systems for online purchases of goods or services. This is a great way to "create" a verified "billing address" for a variety of Financial Privacy techniques. The downside is they only go up to $500.

Although PayPal disallows the purchase of prepaid gift cards, it is possible to buy large quantities of these cards online. There are individuals that sell those for less than the value on the cards sometimes, and there are websites dedicated to the buying and selling of the Visa/MasterCard branded (use anywhere) cards, as well as the department store type cards, iTunes, and etc. Virtually every store has an in-store gift card, including Wal-Mart, Target, and Best Buy. Via the online sites, it is possible to trade, for example, a Wal-Mart gift card for a Visa/MasterCard. In many cases, it isn't necessary for anyone to mail a physical card, as the numbers can be swapped by email, and both sides can call and verify the card's limits. This is a useful tactic for getting cards one may need, in a country where the cards are not physically available.

Prepaid Debit Cards

Prepaid debit cards are similar to gift cards, other than the fact that they can be reloaded, and they require more identity information. The Green Dot card from Wal-Mart can be reloaded at any Wal-Mart, and also registered for online use. Ace Cash Express offers a similar card program, but both request a SSN. The SSN is required in some cases, but the issuer doesn't necessarily ever verify the information as it would not be cost effective to do so. However, if there is ever a problem, they can do it, and if the number is bogus, or doesn't match the name, they could easily disable the card and keep whatever money was loaded onto the card.

Due to the problems with money laundering, and due to the higher limit of $10,000 on this type of card, additional identity information will always be required. With most cards, they sell temporary cards at a retail store, and then once the card is registered the card issuer sends out a new card that is embossed with the registered name entered into the online registration. This can be a valuable technique to acquire a card with a certain name on the card, if no other method is available. However, it is important to note that the card issuer is basically doing a real address verification by physically mailing out the card. A physical address should be considered yet another ID requirement, and another encumbrance to financial privacy.

This type of card is of little use for Financial Privacy, especially as they are usually sold somewhere an individual would have to be on camera to buy them, and reload them. They can be purchased online, but they then require the physical address, a SSN, and a link to some other online payment method via however the card is initially purchased/loaded. As identity theft becomes an increasing problem, the penalties will become more severe in the US, and reduce the value of this type of card further for those that would use it with a random SSN.

Alternatively, if an individual possessed a list of unused SSN, as in non-issued numbers that did not link to an individual, and would never be issued, that may increase the value of this type of card. It bears mentioning that there is a free database online of "dead" SSN. Anyone can verify the SSN of a dead person. The Social Security Administration makes this data public to prevent anyone from using a dead SSN to facilitate a variety of frauds that used to be popular in the US. It is safe to assume that the card issuer has the ability to quickly verify that a SSN from a dead person is being used, although they may or may not flag the card for fraud and disable it until after it is loaded.

Virtual Credit Cards (VCC)

A virtual credit card is simply a number that can be purchased online and used immediately. These are low volume, and rarely heard of or used, so they are not yet attracting unwanted attention from regulatory agencies or law enforcement. Considering they don't show up as a virtual credit card when they are used, they may never show up on the radar. These cards are sold by a variety of specialty sites that can be found linked to virtual currency sites or exchanges. Google can of course provide links to many of these as well. It is somewhat questionable as to whether the virtual credit card (VCC) programs are legitimately supported by the banks that issue them, or if the VCCs are simply a product of aggressive bankers with access to card issuing systems. For the purposes of this book, it doesn't matter.

VCCs can be very useful for online purchases, or untraceable purchases in general. These are often underwritten by Eastern Bloc countries like Estonia, Georgia, Latvia, or etc. In many cases the issuers may appear to be a large and reputable European bank, but actually be issued by a branch office in Serbia. It costs 10% to "purchase" this type of "card". For no-questions-asked, using PayPal, BitCoin, or other virtual currency, a VCC can be purchased online and within 24-hours a card will be created and issued in any name needed. The name on the VCC need not be the same as whatever name is on the actual payment method (BitCoin, LiteCoin, etc.) It is possible to send $1,000 and receive 9x $100 cards that would not be linked together in any way, shape, or form.

The most advantageous use of a VCC is often a built-in special feature: AVS spoofing. A VCC doesn't have an address associated with it, and so a purchase can be made online to ship the product to one address and the Address Verification System (AVS) used by the credit card processor will clear. It is then possible to make a second purchase with a completely different address, and the AVS will still verify as clear. To date, a vendor has not been discovered that even double checked their own database to see if a credit card has verified with multiple addresses, so it is possible to use the same VCC to purchase from a single vendor, and ship to multiple addresses.

The VCC is also very useful for the purchase of online services such as web hosting, proxy rental, virtual servers, or in some cases even doing the initial funding for virtual currency accounts. The 10% is a premium price to pay, but a fair price for full and complete

117

anonymity and financial privacy. As AVS is not even used outside the United States, the VCC is just as useful outside the US. It is also possible to get the VCC numbers online, and using a mag-strip reader/writer to burn physical cards that work perfectly well, but are effectively linked to no one in particular.

Chapter 22: Corporate Structure

Offshore Financial Centers (OFC) are not all created equally, nor do their laws and policies remain constant. As a trend, less and less countries are actually getting on-board with the US failed economic policy, and anyone in finance will readily admit that they realize the US government is on an unsustainable path: it's a mathematical certainty. However, the US has not given up by any means. The current administration has raised corporate taxes to such levels that they have effectively scared off many businesses, and thus the revenue streams that could have saved the country. Now, the US government is grasping at any and every possible revenue source.

The current rhetoric vilifies anyone with money, and the government spins this propaganda with great zeal; "class warfare" it's called. The government is very fond of saying "we just want the rich to pay their fair share", which is ludicrous to anyone with any understanding of economics, but the peasants buy these lines and keep voting for the government that gives them free money. They never bother to contemplate the fact that there isn't enough "rich" to feed them all. Quite simply put, even if the top 1% of the country paid 100% of their wealth to the government, it would only pay the government's expenses for a few weeks. So the poor and the middle-class continue to pay no taxes at all, and the "rich" pay 39.6% of their income so the government can continue to pay their own salaries, while spending just enough on social programs to keep the votes coming in from the peasants that keep them in office.

This broken fiscal policy only puts off the inevitable collapse of the US dollar, and eventual failure of the country. Meanwhile, the US government will do almost anything to keep the lights on, to include breaking all their own laws to seize money wherever they can find it. This policy makes the US the very last place on the planet where one would want to keep money. Unfortunately, 99% of the country is financially uneducated, or simply hopelessly awash with American exceptionalism.

The entire population has a poor understanding of economics due to the fact that the government itself has propagated the sense that "you can always borrow more money". This makes the US a great place to make money, especially for those with international banking relations that enable them to move their profits to safer domiciles. What could be better for business than a whole country of people that believe money grows on trees, and that more credit is just a few clicks away?

The problem with doing business in the US is that the government expects businesses to pay the government's bills with any profits they may make. With an effective corporate tax rate of 39.6%, plus property tax, sales tax, FICA, Medicare, Medicaid, Unemployment Insurance, Workman's Comp, and etc. More than 50% of corporate profits made in the US can be eaten up very quickly. The tax rate for high-net worth individuals is just as bad, but anyone with any measured amount of wealth knows they have to incorporate to enable themselves to take advantage of a greater range of deductions. Owning anything "personally" in the US is now a badge of ignorance, as it easily doubles the total-cost-of-ownership of almost anything.

It is essential to utilize a Subchapter-C corporation (Full Corporation) to not only provide asset protections, but to reduce tax exposure. Even with a holding corporation setup to maintain ownership of expensive items, any money flowing through US banking systems maintains an increased exposure to taxing authorities, law enforcement, and regulatory commissions; which is why it is absolutely necessary to establish banking relationships with at least one Offshore Financial Center, if not several.

C Corporations

In order for a US business to move money abroad effectively, a US corporation is required. Many books have offered up the Limited Liability Company (LLC) as the Holy Grail of Asset Protection, but it is now of negligible value for that purpose. The phrase "limited liability" sounds nice, but what that means is "per manager". Full corporations have officers and shareholders, and thus separate ownership and control from that of the management of the corporation. A LLC is made up of "managers" that simply divide up the responsibility, and tax exposure in their personal capacity. That's to say that a Subchapter-C is a real independent corporate entity unto itself, as where an LLC is a vehicle for several people to divide personal responsibility.

S Corporations

In an S-corporation (the "S" is for small) and a LLC, the tax exposure and liabilities both pass-through to the individuals on the corporation's filing listed as managers. Many lawyers push LLCs from Nevada, Delaware, and New Mexico as "anonymous", but that simply isn't true. New Mexico and Wyoming do not list officers or managers publicly, but the information is still sitting in state files should the government need it. Nevada now only allows the company to be setup without listing the officers, but the officers do have to be entered by the first annual filing. Either way, every US state requires a publicly listed Registered Agent regardless. There is no such thing as an anonymous corporation in the United Sates, and all states will always comply with federal laws and subpoena. Either way, US corporate structure alone can't provide real asset protection.

LLC

A LLC is of negligble value for almost any purpose, but a Subchapter-C corporation can be a valuable component of an international structure that does provide real asset protection. As a corporation has shareholders that bear no personal responsibility for the corporation, they can be anywhere. Since international investments are allowed and encouraged in the US, an offshore company can own and operate a US corporation. Many large US companies actually are owned by international corporations: Motorola (Israel), lkea (Sweden), Nokia (Finland), and of course all the Asian and European auto and electronics manufacturers. This type of setup is completely legal. The US allows this in order to foster international trade, with hopes of money coming into the US, but the corporations send money both ways as is needed for their operations.

Due to the personal liability aspects of an S-corporation, or a LLC, there must be a US "manager" on the hook for an S-corp or LLC. For a C-corp, there still has to be a US Registered Agent, but it is acceptable to have non-US officers, and shareholders. In fact, a US corporation can be owned by an offshore corporation, and thus negates any personal responsibility. This allows the corporation in the US to function independently, provided it complies with US laws. Television, Radio, and any form of legacy broadcast media must maintain 51% US ownership, but all other industries can have complete foreign ownership.

The perceived downside of a full C-corp is the dual-taxation myth. A full corporation does have to file an 1120 tax form in the US once per fiscal year, but payroll is fully deducted from profits, so there is no dual taxation on profits. In fact, with the corporate deductions available, it is almost always more cost effective to operate as a C-corp versus all other types of corporate structures, provided that the company is at least large enough to make it worth the slight additional administrative hassles. For Financial Privacy and Asset Protection purposes, the occasional tax filing is a minor inconvenience compared to the benefits.

Chapter 23: Offshore Financial Centers (OFC)

Offshore Financial Centers operate banking systems for the benefit of an international customer base. In most cases local clients are excluded and unwanted. For example, if an International Business Corporation is opened in the Bahamas, the charter within the corporate documents will specifically exclude business in the Bahamas. The Offshore Financial Centers offer a variety of banking services, and in most cases an increased level of privacy and security, but that is strictly to attract international money. Almost all Offshore Financial Centers segregate their local banking from their international offerings. It is not their intent to promote the corruption of their local business practices with the reduced identity requirements that they offer for international clients. So, opening an offshore bank account is not as simple as going offshore, and then walking into the first bank you encounter. Most Offshore Financial Centers require and/or encourage the use of what is referred to in the industry as the Introduction Service.

The Introduction Service

An Introduction Service is usually a law firm local to the offshore banking community. To use the Bahamas as an example, Nassau Boulevard extends down the leeward side of the island (the west side in this case). This road has a fair amount of tourist attractions, but every other building for several blocks is an Introduction Services or offshore banks. The law firms often advertise Corporate Setup, and Banking Assistance, but they all offer the complete package; they will accept payment from a foreigner, create an International Business Corporation (IBC) registered in the Bahamas, perform the necessary registered agent services, and accept all associated duties with the management of the corporation for an annual fee.

Once an IBC is established, the lawyers will accompany their new client across the street or next door to any number of offshore-only banks, and provide the bank with everything needed to setup a new account. In many cases, the law firm will put themselves down as officers of the corporation, and provide their client with undated signed letters of resignation should the client ever desire to manage the IBC themselves, or to change law firms. The idea is that every document or record associated with the IBC links back to the law firm, and not the individual who owns the corporation. The law firm, in effect, has full Power of Attorney to manage the corporation's affairs, including banking. In the cases of the Bahamas and the Cayman Islands, neither country is a real tax haven any longer. Both work with the United States' Internal Revenue Service (IRS), which is a bit ironic since the Caribbean is of course external to the United Stated.

As of 2013, US citizens could feasibly pay a law firm in the Bahamas to manage a bank account for them, but the practice is discouraged and a client's rights are no longer as effectively protected by law. Both the Bahamas and Cayman Islands are excellent choices for 1st-Level Financial Privacy as they are respected banking hubs for US companies doing business with Caribbean or Latin American nations, but these islands are no longer one-stop-shops for Financial Privacy and security.

Choosing an Offshore Financial Center

Typically Offshore Financial Centers go through phases. A nation with economic problems will open its doors to international banking with reduced regulations and reporting requirements. The money will flow in, and the country will prosper. Eventually the word will get out, and the dirty money will show up. After years of ducking and dodging the US government's anti-privacy policies, most countries eventually give up and sign an information sharing agreement with the US. Panama was a huge Offshore Financial Center until 2009 when the Sanford Bank implosion forced Panama to do a deal with the US. Panama passed a deal that allowed all banking clients two years to get their accounts in order, or get out. Billions simply moved to Guatemala, making Guatemala a new Offshore Financial Center, leaving Panama a fully compliant banking center.

The best practice in most cases is to send money to and from the US via a fully compliant banking environment such as the Bahamas, the Cayman Islands, or Panama. However, for maximum security, the money should only pass through these fully compliant banking environments to a much more private banking environment. Many countries offer very private banking policies, however, each would cause a great deal of suspicion if a large transaction was to occur to or from the US directly. Therefore, it is necessary to use multiple offshore banking relationships for maximum financial security and privacy.

Citizenships & Offshore Banking

Once a banking relationship is established in the Bahamas or a similar fully compliant domicile, it would be advantageous to create an account in a domicile that does not work with the US at all. There are many countries that fall into this criteria. However, it's important to understand that if the bank account is opened by an individual with a US passport, and thus is obviously a US citizen, there are very few banks that will still fail to recognize requests from the US government. It would be an extremely amateur move for a US citizen to open an offshore bank account with their personal identity, and thus very few banks will go out on a limb to protect someone so reckless. The ideal way to open an offshore account is by utilizing a foreign citizenship, in a third country. For example, with a passport from Mexico, Haiti, or Dominica, one could easily open a bank account in Guatemala, Uruguay, or Antigua. This creates a very bullet-proof form of banking secrecy and financial privacy.

The aforementioned countries do not tax internationally derived income, so Mexico wouldn't call a bank in Uruguay and ask about their citizen's account. If the US were to call, the bank has been given all the plausible deniability it needs to disregard any request from the US. They can simply say "due to the fact that you are inquiring about an account with no association to a US citizen or corporation, we hereby respectfully decline to respond to your request due to our security policy". In reality, US law enforcement and taxing authorities know these calls are a waste of time, so they rarely bother to even try. The point is, offshore banks can blow off the US if they are given the resources to do so. Whenever possible, a non-US passport should be used to open offshore bank accounts. If that isn't possible, there is another way to do it.

Using Nominees for Banking

As previously discussed, it is possible to setup a relationship with a law firm to manage an offshore banking relationship. In some countries, this is especially easy, as they allow for "bearer shares". In this case, instead of a law firm or country knowing who owns a corporation, and that information possibly being subpoenaed or publicly displayed, these countries allow the issue of bearer certificates. Whoever holds the certificates, owns the company. This gives the law firms and banks a much higher degree of plausible deniability. In this case the lawyers at the introduction service firm give the client the bonds and undated letters of resignation, and they themselves act as officers of the corporation. The only link to the individual would be the signed management agreement in the law firm's files. As that is globally protected under international law (attorney-client) that relationship remains secure. This is the only safe method for a US citizen to open an offshore account in a non-compliant country, and it's still nowhere near as safe as simply picking up new citizenship just for banking.

Either way, it is never a good idea to send money directly to non-US-compliant countries. The money needs to pass through a fully compliant non-US country like the Bahamas first Money returning to the US needs to traverse the same path in reverse.

Once an offshore corporation and bank account has been established in a non-compliant country, it is still necessary to keep up with the physical bearer bonds/certificates. It would be poor operational security to keep these in one's personal possession, or within that same country. Ideally these would be stored in a safety deposit box in a completely different country, or in a safe located within a fully-owned piece of real estate in a safe area of a safe country. Again, whoever possesses the bonds, could in effect take over the corporation's assets. That would not be a quick or easy process, but it could be done. Therefore, it is essential to physically protect these documents however necessary.

In the US there is now a "Whistleblower Law" on the books. If an individual turns in someone else for tax evasion or fraud, they can actually receive a percentage of what the government is able to recover. So even in spite of their best efforts, many creative businessmen get picked off by ex-wives, girlfriends, business partners, and even their own accountants and financial advisors. This alone should cause anyone with wealth to take great care in the effect of Operational Security. Obviously, if a businessman tells his new girlfriend (a stripper) that he has this great scam he makes millions from, he deserves to lose the money and go to jail. But the system is much more complicated than that due to technology.

It is a very simple matter for any US federal agency to push a few buttons and see what any US citizen filed on their taxes the previous year, and it's quite easy for them to view personal credit reports. If an FBI or IRS agent saw that an individual was making regular payments on a Mercedes and a BMW of near $2,000 a month, and that both cars had insurance and were presumably using gas, that's $30,000 a year. If that individual reported only $40,000 on his taxes, and lives in a nice home, that's an instant red flag. There is no such thing as good police work. Today, criminals are targeted based on financial analytics, electronic communications, and very little human intelligence.

If a businessman is spending his time in strip clubs, casinos, and entertainment venues disproportionately to his industry, then it's suspicious. It's essential to maintain ownership of everything via holding corporations, and to only spend money on entertainment through temporary expense accounts. Any association with wealth, with what appears to be a wage earning tax payer, or worse a tax evader, will eventually result in a visit from the US government. It is no longer possible to live a cash-based lifestyle in the United States, nor is it possible to prevent the documentation of assets. Even if it was possible to buy a Ferrari with cash in the US, the car will be in a database somewhere, and eventually an algorithm will notice that the vehicle has not been declared as an asset or taxed properly.

Chapter 24: Avoiding the Algorithms

It is important to understand the pain-points for banks. At the end of the day, banks just want to make money, but they realize if they allow drug dealers to deposit duffel bags full of cash that eventually banking regulators will shut them down. Each client must keep in mind that the bank is constantly juggling the risk/reward ratio for each questionable client. If the client is profitable for the bank, and not a hassle, the odds are that the bank will do their best to protect that client.

Banks will shut off a "free" checking account for almost any reason, but they would certainly cut some slack for a large corporate account with an average balance of $50,000 and a number of monthly international wires that provide revenue for the bank. In most cases, the dreaded Suspicious Transaction Form can be cleared up in a phone call, or with the fax or email of a little paperwork. That being said, it is essential to be a fully legitimate business and act accordingly, or to fully emulate a legitimate business in every way.

For example, if the business banking client is a check cashing business, the bank expects to see the deposit of large numbers of checks, and to see large cash withdrawals. If the banking client is a casino or vending company the bank would expect to see a large amount of cash deposits, and little or no cash withdrawals. Convenience stores also deal in a lot of cash; as do some smaller grocery stores. Depending on the business model, the parameters will vary widely. When setting up a bank account, it is important to set the proper expectations for the bank, and then only change those slowly over time if necessary. Keep in mind, the longer a bank account has been open without problems, the more secure it is in the eyes of the bank. Thus the inherit value of an aged bank account. The downside of that equation is that the longer any banking activity has been constant, the more suspicious any radical change to the banking activity will be.

Fortunately, the opposite is true as well. If a banking client explained that they had a loan from an international private equity company, or any form of venture capital arrangement, it would be perfectly normal for that client to wire $80,000 to the Bahamas every month; the same amount, and at the same time every month. These electronic transactions would be fully documented on both ends, and thus the bank is in the clear, so to speak. Worst case scenario, the bank could ask to see copies of the loan docs, which they'd add to their files. Loan repayment is a near perfect "excuse" for large transfers, as loan payments aren't taxable to begin with, and the interest is fully deductible as well. Generally speaking, the US government is thrilled when international companies invest in the US. Only the banking client would know that there was no loan, and that the $80,000 payment per month is actually the raw profits of a US domestic venture, if that was the case. As long as the bank has the loan docs on file, they are covered, so it is unlikely that bank security would ever raise a red flag for this small amount of money going to a fully compliant banking center once a month. A savvy Financial Privacy advocate could easily establish dozens of such banking relationships to push out any amount of money.

If someone was to take an interest in the statistical analysis of each and every individual that had great wealth, and they failed to keep it, they would find that these people have much in common. One such common trait would be an encounter with US law enforcement, a US regulatory agency, or a US taxing authority. It is essential that anyone with money understand that the United States of America is a police state and that the US government will use any excuse to seize the wealth of almost anyone. That being said, it's quite easy to blend in with the scores of legitimate businesses, even if the money earned is illegitimate, or derived from some gray area of the economy. As of 2012, the US FBI estimated that 66% of the US economy was off-the-books, illegal, and representative of the underground economy. This is probably a very low estimate, as most organized criminal operations don't fill out surveys for the FBI.

In the US there are millions of inmates being held for the violation of a library of laws that are simply beyond the comprehension of the average citizen. The US currently has a larger percentage of its population locked up than any other country in history. Basically the laws are written in such a way that the state and federal governments can find anyone that they desire to target in violation of some law or another. There is no way to out-smart an arbitrary system that routinely targets the innocent to begin with. Today, it is quite common for the US government to create conspiracies and sweep in large numbers of innocent people by simply coercing confessions from the innocent. This happens every single day in every federal district.

At first glance, this may seem like an impossible game to win, but in reality the fact that the government relies so heavily on those techniques leaves huge holes in the system. For example, a lone individual operating in a city where he knows no one, and no one knows him, doesn't show up on the radar. If this individual wraps himself in a corporate structure, and appears to all the world to be a regular businessman, then he simply blends into society. Using business debit cards to pay for life's expenses, this individual could quite easily duck the pervasive government monitoring systems effectively as well. Obviously this individual could provoke a law enforcement encounter by being flamboyant, or associating himself with lower criminal elements (drug users, prostitutes, or etc.) but otherwise, as long as the individual runs his operation independently, he should be able to successfully manage any activity around the watchful eye of the police state.

Using a Holding Company for Vehicles

One of the most difficult tasks associated with wealth is spending the money. It may seem easy, but the more wealth one has, the more avenues appear for the individual to spend the money. To further complicate the issue, many transactions in the US can draw unwanted attention swiftly. For example, offering to pay cash for an expensive vehicle is a classic mistake. The appropriate way to buy an expensive car is to do a corporate lease through a US holding company that is 5 years old, has good credit, and is in a good state for Subchapter-C incorporation. Paying off the vehicle is another mistake. A paid-off car can be seized, a car with a lien on it cannot. Therefore, even if you put $30,000 down on the lease of an $80,000 vehicle to get the deal done, it's still a lease as long as $1 is owed on it.

Setting up a holding company in Nevada, Wyoming, or many other states is quite easy. It's often possible to franchise in an offshore corporation. The net effect is the convenience of a US corporation, with the anonymity of an offshore corporation. This company can register ownership of cars, buildings, boats, and aircraft that an offshore company cannot. To add security, the holding company could own the vehicle, and then lease it to a corporation in another state. This way a Texas vehicle would show up registered to a Texas business leased to a Texas business, yet the ownership would remain with the Nevada holding company. This can be ideal to reduce law enforcement interaction, while fully protecting the vehicle from seizure, no matter what the Texas company does with it.

Using a Slush Fund

In addition to a holding company for physical assets, a slush fund can be used to shield day to day expenses form scrutiny. It is a simple process to salvage an aged shelf corporation, or incorporate a new company, then add a website, and create all the necessities of a real business. Once this company looks like a legitimate consulting company, it just needs a bank account. From that point it only requires a little bit of paperwork to document this consulting company's "loan" from a friendly offshore corporation. Once a single large transfer has been documented, a businessman could carry a debit card for this company, and/or wire money via a smart phone to pay for any expense; even those that would look suspicious otherwise. Who's to say what a legitimate expense is for a consulting company?

The idea is to create this separate company in a vacuum, ,and not to tie it to any individual or any other company, minus the offshore funding source. That way this bank account can be used for this "anything goes" company, for any purchase. The company will eventually draw the attention of the IRS for not paying taxes, or not filing taxes, at which point any money in the account could be seized. However, smaller companies are only supposed to file taxes once a year in the US. So, considering the filing delays and such, a company setup like this could be run for 12 months, then replaced, giving a businessman almost unlimited access to cash and available funds for random purchases. The downside is that the company must stay below $500,000 to avoid quarterly filing requirements, but a businessman could of course open several of these accounts. Either way, these should not be used for large purchases, that's what a holding company is for. This type of slush fund company should be used for all little (under $1 0,000) purchases needed.

Understanding the Law of the Land

Although this book should not be used as a substitute for legal counsel or common sense, there are certain elements of the law that must be addressed here. Many of the aforementioned techniques could be used for illegal purposes, especially within the United States where the legal system is designed to separate the wealthy from wealth. That being said, there is a legal way, even in the US, to do almost everything covered here. Even so, legal or illegal is no longer black and white, and more gray-area than it is anything else. Today district attorneys practice selective prosecution, and law enforcement agencies have been forced to pursue the least expensive paths to indictments and arrests. It's all about the money, and politics, and less about legal and illegal. There are many crimes that aren't even prosecuted, and some legal business practices that almost always evoke trumped up charges by the US government.

Chapter 25: Best Practices

With the above in mind, anyone of intelligence must consider their position carefully. On one hand, it's illegal to lie about one's income on a mortgage application, it's a federal crime in the US. On the other hand, the banks encourage it, and it's almost never prosecuted. The federal regulations on banks have become so tight that they almost have to fudge the numbers to do loans now, and if the bank can't loan money, they can't stay in business. Yet, when the banks fail, the government has to bail them out. The point is, the system is broken, and one must do what they have to do with their own code of ethics, morals, and values without letting a broken government choose what is right and wrong on their behalf. So within gray areas of the law, it's better to rely on common sense and statistical analysis versus a strict interpretation of the law.

It is important to understand how the system actually works, and not base your decision on how the system is supposed to work. The latter path will lead to constant disappointment. That being said, it is never a good idea to oppose a government head-on. For example, marijuana is legal at a state level in some states. If the owner of a dispensary was to be raided by a federal SWAT team, resisting while screaming "but it's legal" is a mistake.

Therefore, it is the best course of action to not only try to obey the laws of the land, but to always appear to do so even when actually doing so isn't possible or desirable. Only a fool would follow the letter of the law without question, but one would be a bigger fool to openly oppose the laws of a standing government. If the laws must be broken, then it is wise to be creative, exercise great caution, and do so with the required discretion.

Due to the glorification of criminals in the US, the media has effectively used clever subterfuge to convince drug dealers to announce their illegal occupation via gold chains and customized automobiles. The most successful "criminals" on Earth wear Italian suits in office buildings in Latin America or Moscow. At their level, crime is just business. It's hard to have an ethical dilemma over the laws being broken by someone 100 people down the chain-of-command from yourself, especially if those are arbitrary laws in a faraway country. It's a popular notion for Americans to believe that the Latin American cartels are the very essence of evil, an opinion supported by the popular media. Yet Americans conduct

135

business every day that directly supports abominable industries abroad.

As an American, if the purchase of an iPhone doesn't cause any concern for the child labor that produced it, then all rights are forfeited to expect the heads of Latin American cartels to care about drug addiction in America. Countries like Columbia rose up from the 3rd world, and took over positions in education, healthcare, and agriculture far ahead of the US. That money came from US drug users, and reinforced their economy. Meanwhile, Americans use their smart phones to exchange cat videos, and to play Angry Birds.

We are all the center of our own universe, but only a fool will stand in his country and say "this is the best place on Earth", when it's the only place on Earth he has ever been. To be successful today, you have to look at the global economy, and to make investments without nationalistic prejudice. It's also extremely important to recognize that the laws of one nation do not mean any one thing is right or wrong. The law in Saudi Arabia prohibits women from driving cars, yet some untraveled women there no doubt think that it is the best place on Earth. So someone in the US, the country with the most restrictive laws on Earth, should be very cautious allowing those constraints to limit their income potential. What's illegal in one country may be good sport in another. Understandably, it may be necessary to stay in one country for a period of time to make the money needed, in order to finance a life somewhere more agreeable later.

Understanding the Math

In spite of the fact that the United States of America has a horrible economy, massive federal debt, rising unemployment, increasing levels of poverty, and a statistically high level of incarcerated citizens, some people will choose to live in the US. Anyone that has traveled internationally would be quick to point out that the US offers literally nothing that can't be found elsewhere. In spite of the obvious fact that Wal-Mart, McDonald's, and Starbucks exist in almost every country, many US citizens that have not traveled have extremely distorted views of the rest of the world. This is a very common occurrence with individuals that did not come from wealth and privilege, and thus this malformed opinion of the world often holds would-be successful people in a loop of failure; living in an area with the worst economic conditions in the first world, telling themselves it doesn't get any better.

The "American Exceptionalism" is aggravated by the failed public education departments of the US. Any high school graduate of a good school in Latin America can name the countries on the American continent (North, Central, and South America) and yet most Americans couldn't tell you where on planet Earth Nicaragua is. To be successful in today's free market economy, it is impossible to narrow focus to only the US market, and it's a ridiculous concept to only do business in the country with the highest taxes, the most government corruption, and the worst economy. The above are not opinions of the author, these are mathematical facts cited in any of a number of financial publications each and every day.

It should also be pointed out that even if it was possible to set aside all of the above, the US is still the most expensive country to live in, minus maybe the city of Moscow, or London. Not only does the government take a cumulative rate of over 50% of wealth earned in the US, but US citizens continue to use the rapidly devaluing US dollar to purchase more and more expensive items. Everything about the US is hard-wired against people with wealth.

Meanwhile, billionaire Facebook executives and tens of thousands of others that are good at math, leave the US every single year. The year 2012 was the first time in 40 years the US had negative immigration with Mexico; more people traveled to Mexico from the United States, than traveled to the United States from Mexico illegally or otherwise. Mexico currently has half the unemployment rate of the US, and the US rate is seriously padded by changes in the calculation algorithms made by the US Bureau of Labor Statistics; they only count the people currently getting unemployment benefits, not those living off their savings, not those that can no longer get unemployment benefits, not dual income families that are now single income, and not the people that have lost good jobs that are now underemployed.

In short, almost everything is cheaper almost everywhere else. Conditions are ripe for growth in many other locations on Earth, but many xenophobic Americans will miss those opportunities, and life experiences, simply because they "bought the hype"; the lie that has been sold to the American people, that the US is the land of the free (with the highest percentage of its citizens incarcerated in history), and home of the brave (after 10+ years of failed Middle East wars and thousands of servicemen and women have been killed to no avail). It is fully understandable to believe these lies, if the truth was not available. For example, North Koreans have been easily led to believe that they live in the "Worker's Paradise" via their restricted access to the outside world. With the Internet virtually in the hands of almost every US citizens, with broadband covering almost 70% of the US, there is no excuse to live the lie any longer.

However, it is understandable that some US citizens may find reasons that requires them to reside in the US for some period of time. If that's the case, then it is absolutely essential that they understand the risks and take every precaution necessary, regardless of the great inconveniences of doing so.

Understanding the Risks

Living in the US involves the involuntary participation in a variety of systems that allow a high level of oversight by the government: taxation, social security, and now federally mandated healthcare. It's certainly possible to be poor, homeless, or even a college student and not be noticed for failure to participate. There is a huge group of petty criminals, drug addicts, illegal immigrants, and assorted felons that make up America's "underclass", and these people can also quite easily fail to participate. What do they have to lose either way? But with wealth, there is scrutiny, and the expectation to be registered with, and participate in, a variety of government systems. It is important to understand that participation in these systems involves an identity in dozens of databases, and that there are systems in place to look for anomalies in these databases. This isn't science fiction, and this isn't the future, this is the basic computer science behind the systems that have existed for decades.

For example: if an individual had a $500,000 condominium listed in his name, his name would appear next to that condo in the property tax database of his local appraisal district. If the same individual was to register a $100,000 car in his name, that date would appear in the states vehicle registration database, as well as within the database for the vehicles insurance. Both the above transactions would also appear in bank records, and be reported to the regulatory agencies responsible for monitoring US banking. All the above is completely legal and above board, assuming the money used was clean and could be documented. No problem. The problem comes in the first tax cycle, where government computers expect to see someone that can afford such a lifestyle to be making

138

a substantial contribution to the US government in the form of an income tax filing. If no taxes are filed, is it really unreasonable for the government to have an automated script process of all these "anomalies" each year and send them to a government case file system for targeting? It's obviously illegal income, with the added bonus of visible items to seize, which the US government needs to continue to fund their enormous Department of Justice. This isn't a conspiracy theory, this is common sense, basic economics and effective fiscal policy.

Avoiding Scrutiny

Although there is certainly money to be made in the US, the risk is usually not worth the reward. Although all US systems can technically be circumvented by a determined individual, there are no short-cuts. There is no easy way. There is no way to sub-contract the circumvention of the US information gathering systems. But it is possible, provided that the individual has the financial resources to build a corporate framework to support his personal life. It is also necessary to have identification that can be verified via state computer searches, at least in most cases. The idea is to create a life that looks legitimate in every way, no matter where the revenue comes from to support that life. In the aforementioned scenario, there is no way to justify that life. That individual would be living on borrowed time until the government got around to taking a closer look at him. The trick is to not only never show up on those lists of anomalies, but to be able to withstand the scrutiny even if it does happen.

Assuming an individual has access to virtually unlimited money and is not actually employed by a US company, or is otherwise living a life where the information presented here would be most beneficial, he would want to do what he can to change his visible status. Perpetual Travelers with exotic cars, offshore bank accounts, and multiple homes abroad, tend to attract all the wrong kind of attention. As that is exactly the best lifestyle to live, one must work to hide that lifestyle if living in the US. In Cartagena, Cancun, or Barbados this lifestyle is respected, appreciated, revered, and accepted in every way. The working class in these Caribbean paradises will appreciate the fact that you have chosen to spend your hard-earned money within their community.

In the US, you will be targeted by the envious, the lazy, and everyone that has to work for a living. US citizens have a distorted and inflated sense of self-entitlement, and they think they deserve to be wealthy too, even though they haven't taken the first step towards becoming successful. Due to this social conundrum, one must take great care not only to maintain the proper appearance in the databases, but the proper appearance in public as well.

Blending Into the US

The best way to avoid scrutiny from the peasants or their bureaucratic overlords, is to simply blend in with the sheep. That's to say that a middle-management executive making $50,000 a year on a W-2 from a US company, is so common and insignificant, that it invites no unwanted scrutiny. Obviously it's no fun to live at 50K. Who wants to be lower-middle-class? It is not necessary to actually live the lifestyle associated with that tiny level of income, but it is a good idea to take a hard look at the US tax code and see exactly where your comfort level is.

As of the 2012 Tax Code available in 2013, anyone making over $28,250 per year (single, claiming yourself as a dependent) will owe some taxes to the federal government. $50,000 a year is not being wealthy. At that level of income it would be impossible to afford a luxury vehicle, custom suits, or many of the finer things in life, yet you would owe $8,536 to the federal government in the form of income tax just to buy down scrutiny, and this is just the first level needed to maintain the appearance of legitimacy. This is part of the cost of living in the US.

In the scenario above it's perfectly possible to drive a "company car" eliminating the need for the burdensome expense of car payments for this wage-earner identity. It's also possible for this scenario to include a corporate condo, and a corporate expense account. All of the above is perfectly legal. A man can drive a $100,000 BMW M5, and live in a one million dollar condo, with a pocket full of corporate plastic, and still pass the scrutiny of US information systems and public scrutiny. This life is possible, and it could include fine restaurants, lots of toys, and frequent travel. Maybe this identity is an up-and-coming sales rep for a growing company that spares no expense for their best salesmen. This is completely possible, even for a wage-earner that he himself only makes $50K a year. Maybe he's been promised stock options, or some future promotion, for whatever reason he chooses to be employed with this corporation.

Provided the company provides health insurance for the man, and the man's personal bank account reflects regular monthly deposits of $50,000/12= $4,166 (minus withholdings, FICA, Medicaid, and unemployment insurance), this model is doable.

The Cost of Wealth

The lifestyle of a well-to-do sales guy is plausible, and provided the personal identity is kept completely separate from the corporation (the individual isn't a corporate officer) then a reasonably comfortable lifestyle is possible in the US with only a small risk of unintended consequences. That being said, it is not reasonable to expect to drive a Ferrari and live in a ten million dollar home in the US unless every dollar of income is legitimate, taxed, and accounted for. The sheer amount of paperwork and corporate structure necessary to support such an ostentatious lifestyle would be beyond a mere burdensome few weeks of work.

To successfully manage a "rock star" lifestyle in the US with untaxed or illegal income would require a holding company with a full staff to manage its quarterly filings and banking. Ideally the home would be owned by some real estate company, and listed as "for sale" and thus not necessarily inhabited. It may also be possible to write down the value of the home, but either way the property taxes would exceed $200K a year, and a man making $50K a year obviously can't pay that. The numbers have to work. If they don't, then living in the US will be done on borrowed time, and one day the government will send out their agents to seize everything they can.

Chapter 26: Citizenship & Travel

It is unfortunate that having wealth is so expensive in the United States. Money sitting in a US bank account may only make 1% in interest per year, and still be taxed at 39.6%. Every luxury item is heavily taxed, necessitating that these items be corporate owned in order to allow for the widest ranges of deductions. For example, maybe the company that owns the ten million dollar home would spend $500K making an informational video to advertise the home, and thus could write-off the advertising expenses. But either way, living really well is simply not cost-effective in the US. By contrast, a condo on the white sands of the Caribbean Sea in Cancun, Mexico would be taxed at the national rate of only 1%. International wealth is respected, but in the US, the country as a whole attempts to tax the wealth back to middle class status. To live like a rock star there is always Singapore, Macao, Hong Kong, Monaco, or anywhere in the Caribbean, but in the United States of America that lifestyle is best left to actual rock stars.

Using a Passport in the US and Abroad

By this point even the most loyal US patriots have to have come to the conclusion that it would at least be a good idea to take a look at life outside the US. There are a plethora of unfounded misconceptions about international travel. Such as: it is impossible to obtain a passport with a felony conviction that it's impossible to travel while on Federal Supervised Release, and that certain countries do criminal background checks before allowing US citizens access to their countries.

All of the above are myths. Although it may be difficult to get Australian citizenship with a prior US felony, that would only be the case if the crime was a felony there as well, and that's only an issue for citizenship applications, and not a travel visa. Generally speaking, it's easy to leave the US and go almost anywhere. Due to the United States' perpetual war against Islamic nations, there are many countries where an American may not feel welcomed, but very few countries bar entry entirely.

Any US citizen can (and should) obtain a US passport. After the US Patriot Act a second form of photo ID is necessary for many tasks anyway. The benefit of using a passport for ID versus a driver's license is simple, a passport doesn't have a home address on it. It would be an inconvenience to carry around a passport due to its size, so the US State Department now offers a passport card, which is the same size of a regular ID card. It's technically only accepted from Canada and Mexico for reentry into the US, but otherwise it's a well-received form of ID almost anywhere. The process is fairly quick and easy, with a 3-day expedited process available for an additional expense.

The Path of Least Resistance

The US passport is certainly needed to reenter the US, but it is not needed to actually leave the United States. Traveling by air, a passport is usually expected as it would be assumed that one may wish to return to their country of origin. The same applies to travel by cruise ship, but anyone can charter a boat to take them anywhere without a passport. Additionally, it is quite easy to simply drive into Mexico from the US. Mexico has two paths of entry at each border crossing. One is for US citizens that need a travel visa, insurance, passport service, or other official paperwork. There is also a separate path such as Puente Dos in Laredo, Texas. This bridge is in place for Mexican citizens returning to Mexico, and US citizens that merely wish to enter the country for the day to shop, and they do not intend to travel past the 13-mile mark towards the interior of the country.

Northern Mexico is sparse, and rural, minus a few border cities such as Nuevo Laredo (borders Laredo, Texas), Matamoros (borders Brownsville, Texas), and Reynosa (border McAllen, Texas). These Mexican cities were riddled with drug war violence before the election of a new Mexican president, in 2012, that has taken a different stance on the drug war. Although the border towns are much safer, they still lack the high rise buildings and advanced infrastructure found in Mexico City, Guadalajara, or Monterrey. Monterrey is Mexico's second largest city, located less than two hours from the US border. If a US citizen ever needed to leave the US on short notice, and get to somewhere with all the resources of a major US city (and then some), Monterrey would be an excellent choice.

It is quite easy to leave the United States by land, sea, and even air in certain circumstances. Although international air travel via commercial airlines usually does involve a ridiculous amount of security and scrutiny, chartered private aircraft may include little or none. Mexico is of course one of the only two options for travel by land, but the entire Caribbean is open for travel by boat or plane. There is a passport service office at some large marinas and airports, but the vast majority of small airports and marinas in the Caribbean, Mexico, and Central America are wide open. No one wants to blow up anything in the Bahamas, so they don't need or want the same level of security the US has for entry.

To date, there have been exactly zero terrorist attacks in the Caribbean. It's perfectly reasonable to expect to be able to take your private plane or yacht to any Caribbean island, and skip the passport service office. In most of the Caribbean nations the "travel visa" is a simple formality anyway, and really only used so the country can calculate their tourism stats, and not so they can "check out" visitors. In Mexico the FMT (tourist visa) is paper, and to date, isn't filed anywhere electronically. Most of the planet works the same way, and only the US and a few other countries rigorously enforce access rules.

Traveling As a Tourist

In most cases it is possible to remain in any one country for six months on a single tourist visa. If a traveler decides to rent a condo and live in a Caribbean country, he would only need to leave and reenter the country twice a year to stay on a travel visa. Expatriates in Cancun gather together for "visa runs" into Belize twice a year, usually chartering a bus equipped with a margarita machine. This is a popular custom in many expat communities. There is little reason to have a work visa, or full residency, just to live in a country on perpetual vacation. Life as a Perpetual Traveler (PT) allows for multiple residences, and very little documentation needed for travel, entry, or for life in general. In many cases one may choose to live in a 5-star resort for as little as $100 a day in some Caribbean areas, and never bother with real estate at all. As long as the wealth is kept in a safe country, and access to that wealth is via an offshore debit card, there is almost no place not open for leisurely activity.

In the above scenario, there is true freedom. The countries of the world are open for exploration and enjoyment. This is an excellent method to find new relationships, new business opportunities, and maybe somewhere to establish a more permanent home or base of operations. Assuming whatever source of wealth used can be managed with a laptop via an internet connection, the PT model offers everything one needs to run a remote business with the highest quality of life possible. Life in Singapore or Macao can be a great deal more expensive than the Caribbean, but there are very few countries that put tourism revenue behind security consideration such as the United States must do. Other than mainland China, Russia, or a few countries hostile to the US government (Venezuela, Cuba, North Korea, Iran, etc.) a US citizen can get into most countries as a tourist, with very little formal visa requirements. That's to say, it's possible to show up and get an instant tourist visa. Russia and China do require that a formal visa is acquired previous to allowing entry, but both are possible.

For non-US citizens, with a passport from a Latin American country, or Caribbean nation, almost any country is open, without the obvious suspicions associated with US citizenship. With non-US citizenship, it's possible to travel the world without the US police state documenting each step.

Citizenship and Extradition

At some point a wealthy individual that has made his fortune in the US may choose to fully detach himself from the anchor of US citizenship. There are many options for new citizenships. It's possible to obtain economic citizenships via investing in the economies of other countries. It is possible to obtain citizenship via marriage. It is also possible to obtain citizenship in Ireland, Mexico, Israel, or a few other countries via proof of ancestry from those countries. Many of these methods can take thousands of dollars, and take years. The above are fully legal, and recommended methods to obtaining legal citizenship. If at all possible, and if there would be no problems linking your citizenship from your birth country to a new citizenship, the above is the right method to choose. Any immigration firm can provide advice on the above.

However, if there is a situation where an individual has developed an unhealthy relationship with the government of his birth country, it may be a bad idea to link a new citizenship to the original one. This would especially be true if the individual was wanted in his birth country, or owed a significant amount of money in that country, or to that country. Again, this book is no substitute for proper legal advice, and at no point is the following information intended to advise anyone to break the laws of any particular country. There is no way to provide comprehensive real-time legal information for all 193 countries in print format. Therefore, the

146

following will be provided for informational purposes only.

There are stacks of books with drawn-out and convoluted ways to achieve residency in various countries. Getting a passport in Panama isn't the same as being born in Panama, and the passport will reflect the difference between a foreigner with economic citizenship, and a natural born citizen. So it is perfectly clear, if you were to be arrested in Europe with a Panamanian passport that states you were born in the US, then Interpol will call the FBI, and there is a good chance of extradition back to the US where the laws will weigh against you.

Remember, the US hands out more time for crime than anywhere else, and it is the only country that charges it's citizens for crimes that may have been committed abroad. An $80,000 economic citizenship in Panama will have been a waste of money. Economic citizenships are great to get passports for banking purposes, to own real estate, or to start a business in another country, but it does not disconnect someone from their birth country. If your birth country is Mexico, China, or almost anywhere, it's not a problem. If you were born in the United States, then it is a very big problem, as US citizenship acts as something between a leash and a bungee cord. It is therefore sometimes advantageous to fully disconnect that relationship, or at least pick up a completely disconnected stand-alone citizenship in a friendly country. With a citizenship in a country where wealth is most respected, additional options may become available should there ever be a situation where the scales of justice could be tipped via a well-placed payment.

Alternative Identities

Acquiring real citizenship status in another country, as if you were born there, may seem difficult. In reality, a man or woman can only be born once, and in one country or another, right? Fortunately, reality and history frequently part ways, so although that may be the case, what matters is the documentation. Although identity theft in the US has caused a great number of changes in US identity systems, most countries do not manage personal credit in the same way that makes it profitable to do identity theft. The US also has a Bureau of Vital Statistics that serves the singular purpose of comparing birth certificates to death certificates, and keeping up with who's dead and who isn't. The rest of the planet, minus the United Kingdom, has not made great strides towards becoming quite the Police State the

US has. So in most countries there is little or no correlation between births and deaths, and this creates possibilities for exploitation.

Many years ago a book was published in the US called "The Paper Trip" followed by a second, and third version. It is important to note that there are very few techniques that can be used to gain a new identity in the US, and zero that are legal. That is a fact. Any book or commentary that advises to the contrary is factually inaccurate. Since 9/11 any attempt to create a second identity in the US has been a well pursued felony, and so nothing discussed here should ever be attempted in the US. That being said, these techniques work quite well elsewhere.

In many countries the average citizen may never have or need a passport, and so it becomes possible to obtain duplicate identification documents, have a new passport made, and then to travel. If a rural resident of Mexico has his ID borrowed for the creation of a passport only used outside of Mexico, why would he care? If he did, what could it cost to rent his blessing in the endeavor? Is there a law in Mexico against renting out your identity? These are questions that certainly deserve further consideration. It's a simple fact that millions of citizens of Mexico, Honduras, Guatemala, El Salvador, Nicaragua, Costa Rica, and Panama, exist in rural parts of society where a small payment would be much more appreciated than an identity document that they have no use for. There are of course just as many rural Americans that might sell their identity, but due to the infrastructure of security in the US, these identities are far less valuable.

Chapter 27: A Better Way

In line with good OpSec, a wealthy individual may find it undesirable to make new friends in Latin America, and rent an identity. In this case it would be desirable to borrow an identity from someone who no longer needs it, such as the dead. The most efficient way to undertake this endeavor would be to take a smart phone with a camera to a rural cemetery and find a deceased person with approximately the right year of birth that died at a young age before they would have acquired any additional identity documents beyond the initial birth certificate. Once you have 20 or 30 pictures of the headstones it's a simple process to verify that a death certificate isn't filed with a central government office. In the US there is an actual death registry for this purpose, although most countries have no central death registry, so any birth certificate that doesn't have a full identity already attached to it could be used to get a passport, voter registration, or registry documents.

To get a driver's license it would be necessary to take the driving test. Depending on your age, you may need some explanation as to why you are getting your first driver's license. If you just moved to Monterrey, Mexico from New York, or Mexico City, you could easily say that you have used public transportation your whole life. It's equally possible to explain to anyone that asks that you just moved back to Mexico from the US, and now you need a Mexican driver's license to drive in Mexico, even though you've driven in Wyoming your whole life. You may be able to trade in a Wyoming driver's license for a Mexican one. Needless to say, there is virtually no chance that it would be verified for authenticity.

The above is referred to as "the dead baby" method of obtaining new ID. It is quite easy to solicit the local churches and hospitals for birth records, and there are many law firms that would be happy to accept $100 from a new client, and to send some underpaid paralegal out to retrieve their new client's birth certificate. With the US economy in a free fall, people are leaving the US in droves and returning to their birth countries. More and more services will be launched to help these returning citizens get their identity documents in order. A quick Google search for "Mexican birth certificates" would yield at least one such service, one that allows everything to be handled online. They even accept PayPal payments.

Although Mexico is used in the example, this technique works in many other countries, and will ultimately lead to a perfect passport for not only banking offshore, but for ideal extradition scenarios. That, and Mexico is a respected economic power with significant export capacity, it's a reasonable passport for a businessman to be carrying provided that he speaks passable Spanish. Mexico hasn't gone to war with any Islamic countries, so it's a far safer passport to travel with than a US passport. Depending on your skin color and languages spoken, one of the Caribbean countries may be a more believable birth country for you. The country of Belize borders Mexico, and it's an English speaking country (formerly British Honduras). Belize has also proven to be useful for this particular technique.

Have Name Will Travel

In many countries it is much easier to complete a legal name change than in the US. As the US ties personal credit histories to a Social Security Number, and rigorously polices identity dates, it is an arduous task to change a name. Even so, it is still just a legal process, and there are self-help guides available for those that choose to try their luck of making a name change without a lawyer. Anyone can do it; no country disallows name changes. Therefore, users of the "dead baby" technique would not be married to the name they find for the process. It' s of course tempting to choose a "coo l" name when changing names, but anyone that values wealth and privacy can tell you that's not a good idea.

The best idea is to Google a list of the most popular first and last names for whichever country needed, and then choose from the top five first names and last names. In many Latin countries it would be necessary to choose a mother's maiden name to join with a last name as well, as it is customary. With this technique, anyone looking through the databases to find you would be unable to easily determine which Juan Carlos Garcia you might be. If your ego requires more personal designation then by all means, choose a nickname.

Once a passport with the chosen name is in hand, the best solution for total privacy would be to leave that country, and enter another country on a tourist visa. The US is very xenophobic, with great prejudices against immigrants, in spite of the fact that the country was founded by immigrants that committed sweeping acts of genocide against the indigenous populations of North America. The rest of the world certainly is not as prejudice, or ethnocentric. It is perfectly acceptable for a citizen of Mexico or the Bahamas, to do business in Panama, Colombia, Brazil, or anywhere else. There are tax laws, and visa requirements in some cases, but that is just paperwork and not an insurmountable hurdle to progress.

If an individual really wanted to start a new life, it would be possible to exercise the following steps: dead baby, name change, new country; with a tourist visa, and then dead baby in the new country repeat as necessary. This would produce a number of legitimate passports (that should never be kept in one place) that could facilitate much easier world travel with reduced oversight, and greatly increased financial privacy.

Chapter 28: Combining Resources

When considering countries to travel to for business or banking purposes, it is important to keep in mind international treaties and shared banking charters. It is also important to keep in mind that these things change from time to time, but there will always be certain foundations in the realms of global banking. For example, Switzerland has been a solid banking environment for over 200 years, and through two world wars. The cost of entry is high, as private banking options usually begin with a $100,000 deposit, and unfortunately the Swiss government now has to disclose the financial details of any US citizen to the IRS (or any other agency in the US that requests it). Of course, as has been discussed here, only a novice would open a personal bank account in their name, or any name associated with a US identity. Switzerland is a perfectly safe place for an offshore corporation to bank, as is Dubai, Hong Kong, Singapore, or Lichtenstein.

Europe and Asia are excellent places to store large amounts of money in the Swiss Franc, or any gold-based currency. Dubai is a growing financial power, but as their real estate industry has taken a beating, their banks are less secure than they once were. In many cases these banks may offer somewhat fewer day-to-day services than the Caribbean banks, but having money that is perfectly safe is worth the price of some inconvenience of access. Ideally, these banks in Europe and Asia would be used for long-term storage of money not otherwise invested, or needed for expedient access. For better account access to funds with a higher level of liquidity, the Caribbean offers much better banking services. Using a combination of all of the above would allow a savvy individual to have reasonable access to his money, without sacrificing the security of the bulk of his wealth.

White Card Programs

In this day and age cash is worth so little, and draws too much negative attention, and so access to wealth is usually done via one plastic card or another. For larger transactions it is now possible to wire large sums of money via a smart phone with encryption technology. The Caribbean banks offer excellent online access and smart phone apps for these purposes. Making a large purchase in the US via a wire from outside the US may require additional explanation, but as long as the wire comes from the fully compliant nation of the Bahamas, or the Cayman Islands, then this should at least be possible, although some taxes may be owed for the presumed repatriation of funds. If at all possible, the transfer should be made offshore-to-offshore. In many cases any company in the business of selling luxury goods will have offshore banking relationships setup for just such occasions.

Another option is the white card, or white label debit/credit card. Banks in Cypress and Panama offer this type of service. Basically there is a bank account setup to back a plain vanilla debit card from a non-compliant, or partially compliant, nation that allows the funding for this account to come from anywhere. The Cypriot service allows for almost unlimited "loading", with a per load fee only. The card itself has maximum daily cash withdrawal limits, maximum daily purchase limits, and an open AVS so the card can be used to send internet purchases to any address. As an added bonus, they will print anything on the card desired. This service is very popular with international contractors, as their parent company can just load the employee's card with his pay as often as necessary without exposing the employee to the mercy of the banking laws for whatever country he happens to be in. In these cases the card will often have the corporation's branding on the card, instead of the banks.

If one of these cards were recovered by law enforcement, the card would come back as a prepaid card, not linked to any bank accounts that might actually have a significant amount of money in them. In the case of Cypress, they usually won't even speak to US law enforcement, as their banks deal with a number of Russian oligarchs that have no love lost for US bureaucracy. As of March 2013, Cypress is negotiating an EU bailout, which may or may not affect their service offerings. Either way, most introduction services, and privacy consultants, can guide a businessman towards other white card programs. For the right amount of money, any bank would launch a similar program as needed for a corporate client. It would also be possible to simply setup and use any debit card program from a non-compliant country in the same fashion.

The Presentation of Wealth

As previously established, with wealth comes scrutiny. In many cases that scrutiny will only extend as far as the answer to the question "So, what do you do for a living?" It goes without saying that there should at least be a prepared response for that question, but minus government agents and bankers, it's no one's business to ask. In the case of banks, they just need answers to fill in the blanks on their forms. If someone was to say "I'm a technology consultant for the point-of-sale industry" that doesn't usually segway into deeper conversation. It is a good idea to pick a subject and educate yourself on it if you need to, but you don't need an MBA to convince a banker, that wants to be convinced to begin with, that you are a "host services management consultant", or a "logistics efficiency analyst". The point is, if you have an obscure source of income and millions in the bank, you need to convey an easier to digest lifestyle to lower echelon people. It may be tempting to say "I'm independently wealthy" or "It's none of your business what I do", but these are very bad replies that will only increase scrutiny.

Whoever you are, whatever you actually do, you need an easy to convey persona that leaves no real impression. In a world where the governments and criminals alike have the means to take wealth from the unwary, only a fool would "show off" ill-gotten wealth. It's perfectly okay to drive a Ferrari (especially outside the US), and it's quite acceptable to display obvious wealth if you have a back-story locked in place that can make the source of that wealth obviously legal. It's just important to understand that in today's society being ostentatious, and flamboyant has an extremely high recurring tax, to such a degree that it's simply not worth the trouble in some countries, especially the US.

Outside the US, wealth is much more appreciated. Entire countries depend on tourism revenue from the wealthy and powerful of the world. These are the best countries to live in, on perpetual vacation, even if you actually get some work done while you are there. Even in a friendly country, it's a good idea to have a business card that displays a website that fully demonstrates what appears to be a legitimate company of some kind. In this case the pseudo-company could also be the same company name on the white-cards with your wallet. This adds to the persona of an honest businessman on vacation, or a business traveler working for an international firm. All of the above may seem a bit too James Bond for many people, but if you ever find yourself being interrogated at an international airport, it would be better to be James Bond than someone with no excuse for their luxurious lifestyle.

Attention from the security of an international airport, or even the police, is rare, but you can't discount bad luck. Unless you keep up with world affairs as a full time job, it would be impossible to anticipate many events that may cause additional scrutiny at a country's point of ingress or egress. It pays to be prepared, and even though any grade school kid can make a website these days, a single website is a quick and free way for any random authority figure to check your story. If nothing else, it sets you aside from common criminals, and hopefully whoever it is they are actually looking for. Some people may need to have multiple names, passports, personas, and lifestyles. With the techniques outlined here that's easily possible. It is up to each individual to determine how much privacy and security they need, and to use the tools presented here to secure themselves against would-be threats to their wealth and freedom.

The Rarity Of Wealth

There has been an all-out assault on the social consciousness of the US regarding those that have wealth, and those that do not. The catch phrases often include the term "the 1%" in reference to the wealthy. The peasants screaming their slogans in the streets rarely have the capacity to appreciate that 1% pays over 50% of all taxes, or the fact that they are already paying a disproportionate tax rate. The current US administration is very fond of rhetoric that infers that the wealthy do not pay their fair share. This is likely to continue, as politicians will continue to prefer 99% of the votes versus 1%, even though that 1% employs half the country that is actually working.

The politicians in the US enjoy painting the 1% as super wealthy individuals with summer homes in the Hamptons and a yacht, but 1% of the 350 million people is 3.5 million people. The vast majority of those individuals are surgeons, engineers, and small business owners using DBA, LLC, or S-Corp corporate structures. There are quite a few millionaires participating in the US economy, but today that doesn't mean you can afford exotic cars or a yacht. Most of these millionaires are business owners, or those that manage their money responsibly their whole lives, and have good investments. These are retired people, older citizens, not those driving Ferraris and living the rock star lifestyle conveyed by politicians.

Less than 1.8% of US citizens earn over $100,000 a year, and although there are quite a few citizens with a net worth of over $1 million, there are very few that have $1 million with full liquidity. Again, the vast majority of this wealth is tied up in slow-growth (stable) investment vehicles, real estate, and small business. The list of multi-millionaires is a much shorter list, and the list of multi-millionaires that are under 50 years old is a far shorter list again. Statistically, it's difficult to amass millions of dollars, and it's even more difficult to keep it through good investments. Although this is certainly good to keep in mind when the politicians are on TV proselytizing to the masses, it's a far better idea to keep your wealth somewhere it's appreciated, not demonized.

Working with Big Banks

Considering how rare wealth is statistically, it would be prudent to consider this fact when reviewing options for investment and asset protection vehicles. Since there is such a small customer base for Wealth Preservation/Management Specialists, the industry has always been a bit treacherous. There will always be big investment firms such as Merrill-Lynch and Charles Schwab, but that type of US based service falls short in many areas. They are great for low-yield (safe) investments, especially for the retired. However, if you absolutely needed to stick $10 million somewhere fast before subpoenas are issued by the attorney of an ex-spouse, then Merrill-Lynch can't help you. If those subpoenas are coming from the US Attorney's office then no one in the US can help you. But you can always help yourself, especially if you are well prepared for any threat to your wealth that could possibly occur.

Obviously Charles Schwab doesn't offer offshore banking services, but there are many groups that do. A fair number of these groups are on the shady side, often located in distant parts of the world. There are many legitimate groups such as The Royal Bank of Canada which will be happy to assist you with moving your wealth to one of their tax free branches in the Isle of Man, Jersey, or Guernsey Islands. Each are excellent choices for tax havens. HSBC Bank also offers a variety of offshore services that any US citizen can obtain with a quick trip to any of their offshore branches. The problem is that many report the contents of accounts held by US citizens to the US IRS or any other US government agency that asks for the information.

Although it is still possible for a US citizen to walk in to a bank in some obscure part of the world and safely open an account with cash, that doesn't mean that the bank won't turn the money over to US authorities if asked. Some countries will turn cash over, some will freeze it, and others will do neither, but they will tell the US government anything they happen to ask. It is a good idea to research the International Tax Information Exchange Agreements (ITIEA) between the US and wherever banking is being considered. Walking into a bank with passport in hand is generally a safer solution (at least where financial privacy is concerned) than just dealing with a big bank directly. But this technique lacks the foundational security of the offshore corporation method. Using a nominee trust or offshore corporate structure is always the best solution, even if you are using a one man introduction service versus a multi-billion dollar bank directly.

Chapter 29: Alternative Asset Protection

Precious Metals

The idea of having millions of dollars in a single bank account is appealing. This is especially true if the bank has great online banking, customer service, and interest rates. For asset protection purposes, liquidity works both ways. The money you have easy access to can as easily be liened, frozen, or seized. Here we must reflect upon the historically significant Golden Rule: "He who has the gold, makes the rules". Gold has climbed in value steadily for decades, beating inflation, the S&P 500, and many other indexes. Sure, it's heavy, inconvenient, and frowned upon for major purchases, but it is safe. One could of course buy gold and bury it, which is the oldest form of asset protection, and no doubt still used today. Alternatively, one could purchase gold-backed precious metal certificates, which can be more easily transported or used for other banking purposes.

In the case of physical gold, it is now possible to buy investment grade 1 once bars of gold online, and via local gold and silver exchanges. Most of these places do a plus or minus 3% rate. If you buy gold, you pay 103% of the daily rate for gold. If you sell gold, they pay you 97% of the daily rate; it is a simple business model. You can buy and sell gold anywhere in the world, and although its' around $1,800 an ounce (as of January 2018) and thus not a very portable form of wealth, it isn't a lot worse than cash. One million dollars in US $100 bills is roughly 22 lbs. That same 22 pounds would be $563,200 in gold. The benefit of gold sitting in a shoe box, wall safe, or treasure chest, is that it increases in value as opposed to cash that decreases in value. This makes physical gold a fair choice for the preservation of wealth.

An optimum scenario would involve having gold in safety deposit boxes at an offshore bank that you do no other business with; no other accounts of any kind. This guarantees that no transaction can ever be traced back to the location of the gold. Another option would be to own real estate in countries that always allow easy access with as simple floor safe to store gold in, and maybe additional identity documents if needed. The ultimate solution for hiding gold would be to load it into a heavy container and place it on the ocean floor in 70 to 80 feet of water in a flat area chained to a rock. Assuming you have the ability to use scuba equipment, and GPS to plot the position for future recovery. As long as you are the only human on Earth that knows the coordinates, there is zero chance anyone is going to randomly run across your treasure, and it would still be there decades into the future and even more valuable than when you sank it.

A less extreme means of using gold or silver is the precious metal certificate. There are companies that offer certificates of ownership for any weight of gold or silver needed. These work just like a gold and silver exchange, but they keep the gold or silver. These certificates can be used as currency in some cases, or as collateral for a loan. These differ from simply buying gold or silver from a brokerage account. The ticker symbol GLD and SLV denote a stock price of sorts (an index) based on the metal's floating price. You can buy or sell as often as you like, but you don't actually take possession of the gold or silver, it's just an investment linked to the price of gold or silver.

With a precious metal certificate you have a negotiable instrument that can be used for a transaction, or held in a safety deposit box for future use. In some cases it is possible to make a purchase to have the certificate delivered, or picked up later, so there is nothing in-hand to give up the location of the certificates, provided a payment wasn't made by wire or any other obviously traceable method of payment. In the case above, you would need to physically travel to the company using the certificates, and verify you are the purchaser, to retrieve your certificates. Meanwhile, the gold or silver would continue to increase in value.

Investment Grade Diamonds

Traveling with a lot of gold would be ill-advised and inconvenient. The original point of paper currency was to avoid just that situation. If there is ever a situation where an individual needs to physically load up multiples of millions of dollars and leave a country, cash is not much more efficient than gold. At 22 lbs. per million, one man can't physically carry a real fortune, or even a good retirement. It would be unfortunate to ever have to carry all of your wealth on you, especially for international travel, but it is possible. The solution is diamonds. No, not the diamonds from Zale's or Tiffany's; what is needed is raw investment grade stones. Cut, but not in any form of jewelry. Every major city in the US has several vendors of investment grade diamonds. These vendors are usually located in heavily armored office buildings off the beaten path: not in strip malls, or high rises. You will need an appointment, and you will need to be buzzed-in to get in. In many cases you might need to do some homework and at least take a crash course in color, cut, and clarity (how diamonds are rated), but in an emergency diamonds are the only method to rapidly consolidate multiples of millions of dollars into a portable package that one can carry.

You will also find that many of the diamond brokers will take gold, and other creative payment options. Many also have existing offshore banking relationships, so it may be possible to pay off-shore-to-offshore, without traversing US banking systems. If you need to leave a country fairly rapidly, the US for example, you could easily wire money from the US to a diamond broker's offshore account. Sure, the US side of the transaction would be recorded and the IRS would be alerted. This activity would generate a letter, and maybe even a phone call, but a bank would have no reason to hold up the wire, especially coming out of a corporate account. If you were to return to the US, the IRS would surely freeze a bank account in lieu of a tax filing to explain the transaction, but that could take years. Meanwhile, the diamonds would have passed through airport security, and could be on the other side of the planet.

Fine Art

There have been stories of IRS raids on multi-million dollar homes that turned up completely empty handed. The cars in the garage were found to be leased, and the home itself on an interest-only loan with no equity. The IRS doesn't want to seize pianos, appliances, or anything cumbersome to document, move, and resale. In some of these cases, the agents walked right by priceless art or antiques. In March of 2013 a single Picasso was sold at an auction by Steve Wynn (Vegas casino mogul) for $155 million. That is a significant amount of money to hang on the wall, so having insurance and good security would be a must. The upside of art is that it usually increases in value as well, in relationship to the time of death of the artist. Picasso is no longer turning out any new work, so his pieces will continue to increase in value. Art isn't easily turned into cash, but Sotheby's and other major auction houses have fairly regular auctions. Again, participation in this subset of wealth would require some homework, but it would be very beneficial.

If someone were to purchase millions in art, and then loan the pieces out to museums, the wealth is preserved, protected, and serving a public interest. In this case, it's also not on the walls of the mansion the IRS is visiting either. If you asked the museum to keep the ownership private, they will always do so. The net results of this technique is to hide millions in plain sight, and to preserve wealth in such a way that it increases in value, with little exposure to taxing authorities or litigants. That, and this technique buys caretakers for your wealth, and doubles the insurance and security. The next time you visit a fine art museum look for the tags that say "On loan from a Private Collector". In these cases, it's a safe bet that the piece isn't being fully declared to taxing authorities, if at all.

For an added layer of security it is possible to incorporate an art collection as a business via a holding company type corporate structure. With this technique money is invested in a private company instead of the art directly. The IRS doesn't force the sale of private companies to recover individual investments. Assuming you have full control of the company (via proxy) this technique adds a layer of security for asset protection, without degrading the value or liquidity of the assets held by the corporation.

Private Investments

Setting up a company to open a bank account is the most obvious form of asset protection via corporate structures. Beyond simply having a bank account, a corporation can maintain the ownership of cars, real estate, art work, or even intellectual property (patents, trademarks, etc.). To take it a step further, a corporation could actually be in the finance business. It is perfectly legal for a Bahamian IBC to own a Wyoming Subchapter-C corporation that acts as an investment firm. In some cases the SEC regulates certain aspects of financial services, but a straight investment fund, or hedge fund, requires no registration. This company could quite easily invest via any of the easy-to-use online brokerage services such as eTrade, TDI-Ameritrade, or Interactive Brokers, and only incur the tax exposure for profits taken. As in previous examples, it's almost always possible to get the money out of a hostile tax environment, even if it means the corporation owes taxes later. Those taxes owed would fall on whoever the officers were at the time of the transaction.

That being said, the company could easily make a "bad investment" right in time for the tax year. If the company takes in $10 million to invest, and is worth $11 million at the end of the year, that would be $1 million of tax exposure if the profits are "realized".

However, if the company shifted $10 million into a Dominican Republic banana farm right before the end of their fiscal year, that's a perfectly legal investment even if you own the offshore corporation 's bearer bonds for Dominican Bananas Inc. The object is to keep profits where the taxes are not, and to move your losses over to the domiciles with the highest taxes like the US. This is the same technique large companies like Google use to "avoid" (not evade) taxes. In this case, with the right paperwork, the technique can also be used to move money out of the US tax free.

Aircraft, Yachts, and Exotic Cars

At first glance an airplane may seem like an ideal vehicle for the transportation of wealth. For example, an aircraft could be purchased by a corporation in the US, flown to Belize, and sold. Provided that the aircraft didn't make the conversion from new to used, it should be worth almost the same on both ends. This model works, but it is important to remember that aircraft, yachts, and automobiles all depreciate (minus maybe class/collector cars), thus vehicles make poor asset protection choices.

That being said, if the vehicles are "working" then the math improves. If money was moved into a corporation that has the capacity to rent out aircraft or yachts (not so much automobiles, but possibly trucks) then it would be possible to offset the depreciation with income from the rentals. In this case the vehicles are simply a part of a company's holdings for financial purposes, and subject to the usual fixed-asset depreciation schedules used for US taxation purposes. This is a bad choice for asset protection unless there is an opportunity to pick up aircraft, yachts, or trucks for a good price. Concerning the portability aspects, it is possible to invest almost any amount of money into a single yacht or aircraft, but this would not be possible with trucks or cars. The most expensive car is under $3 million, and all exotic cars depreciate so fast that they actually score as one of the worst asset protection choices.

On the other hand, if one has the ability to pilot his own aircraft, or sail his own boat, then it becomes a very simple matter to move wealth from one country to another. The downside is that aircraft and yachts normally require a lot of due diligence during the sales process, so these items cannot usually be converted to cash.

Chapter 30: The Corporate Veil

In this section asset protection has been detailed utilizing US based corporations to hold assets. Although this is part of a good strategy, it is by no means effective on its own. If a US citizen was to create a new corporation, or worse an LLC, and use the new corporate structure to hold fine art, vehicles, or real estate with themselves listed as the corporate officers and the registered agent, then all they have really accomplished has been to create some additional paperwork for a hostile government agency or litigant. If the company can't show annual minutes, payroll, advertising, and most importantly customers, then it can quickly be declared to be an extension of the individual himself and fully seizable for debt collection. This is called piercing the corporate veil.

In order to maintain the integrity of the corporate veil (in the US) it is necessary to have solid financials, banking history, customer records, and multiple officers and/or owners, even if all of the above is derived from international sources and could not be verified in the US. If your company is legitimately in the aircraft business, then it is unlikely that the corporate veil would be attacked, especially if the company has customers and employees other than the corporate officers. However, if the company is only being used to hold the titles of ownership for assets, then the owner has full exposure in the US.

This is why it is always a better idea to "franchise" a foreign corporation into a US state. This method preserves offshore ownership so the actual "owner's name" doesn't have to appear on corporate filings in the United States. This arrangement would make it very difficult for any US government agency or litigant, as they would bear the burden of attempting to find the true ownership of a foreign corporation. If the government can tie that to a US citizen, then they have the lawful authority to hold that person responsible for taxes, regulatory compliance, and/or civil debt.

Asset Recovery Specialist

The US has whole divisions of agents in various agencies that specialize in asset searches and the forensic accounting used to find the legal ways to encumber or seize assets. They will often seize the physical assets if they can, while they spend months or years trying to find the legal means to keep what they have seized. There are private companies that do the same work for civil litigants and attorneys.

In every case, your wealth, or assets that represent wealth, are more secure outside the borders of the United States. In order for the US government to evoke the assistance from law enforcement in a foreign country they must utilize Mutual Legal Assistance Treaties (MLATS). These are public documents, available online. In some cases a foreign government may only want to be bothered with the United States' problems in cases of murder or drug cartel activity and not civil debt, tax collection, or allegations of fraud. This is the scenario with many South and Central American countries.

Either way, Asset Recovery Specialists have been known to break the rules, whether they are employed by the government or otherwise. For this reason, physical assets that can't be secured fully should be avoided. There is only so much you can do to secure an aircraft at an airport you don't control. In all cases, nothing should ever be in a personal name, and any offshore corporation is better than any US state's corporate structure. Even then, Asset Protection Specialists will lie, cheat, and steal to get information from foreign banks and government agencies.

With that in mind, all transactions should be indirect if you wire money from the US; don't send it directly to Dubai, Hong Kong, Switzerland, or wherever the bulk of your fortune sits. The best practice is to bounce money through the Bahamas or Cayman Islands (the Northern Caribbean route) first, and then on to Uruguay, Panama, Guatemala, or any friendly Caribbean nation. Then it should be moved to a secure domicile in Asia or Europe. Always vary the amounts, and never do same-day transactions. If you wire in $100,000, wiring out 2 wires for $50,000 that same day doesn't buy any security. Bleed it into random accounts over weeks, and then bleed it out. Looking at transaction history, it would be very difficult for an Asset Recovery Specialist to make a case that this was anything but normal business between international corporations, even if he was to somehow get access to it.

The Disclaimer

Throughout this book many subjects have been touched on without a specific how-to being presented. The reason for this is simple: regulations, rules, and laws change. Knowing how all the moving pieces work together is a great deal more useful than any current loophole in the system. However, to deliver maximum value to those that have purchased this book, some examples here have been included in the following pages. These techniques are tried-and-true, and have worked well for years, but it would be a good idea to do your homework all the same in case something has changed.

These are hypothetical "what-if" scenarios for informational purposes only. As a disclaimer, no one should actually try to utilize these very effective techniques, for any reason. Although these examples may use the US as a starting point, it does not mean that these same techniques would be any more or less effective in the UK. That being said, if anyone were to execute any of the following strategies outlined they could very well be in violation of the laws of one nation or another. It is not the author's intent to validate the laws of any one country as morally or ethically righteous. Each and every human being on Earth should make his or her own decisions in regard to obeying the laws of a nation. However, from a strictly logical position it should be noted that if you have an inability to abide by the laws of your current country of occupancy, it would be a good idea to relocate to a country more in line with your personal code of ethics.

The Big Bag of Cash Scenario

In this hypothetical example, let's assume that you have worked extremely hard your whole life trying to make ends meet, and you haven't been able to amass true wealth in a safe domicile. In fact, let's assume that you are so down on your luck that you have decided to spend the rest of your tiny savings on a week long vacation alone at a lake-side cabin. While investigating a noise in the attic of this cabin, which turns out to be rats, you discover a large duffel bag of cash; several million dollars. At this point you should probably, by law, contact the owner of the cabin, and the police. [This is your legal notice]. As you can tell via the cobwebs that the bag has been there a few years, let's assume that you make the logical decision to keep the money as most people would.

Now, you have many problems. Getting caught with unexplainable cash in the US can mean a lengthy visit to a county jail. You have no idea if the money came from a bank robbery, the Mafia, the Vatican, or from big foot. All you know is that you have a bag full of large denomination bills held together by rubber bands. For the point of our hypothetical example, we'll assume the bills are not sequential, or marked in any way. Your first thought is to load the bag into the car and take it home, but then you remember reading this book, and instantly realize that a single highway patrol stop for anything could land you in jail. And so, here's what you actually should do assuming you are not breaking the laws of your town, city, county, state, or country to do so, right?

You take several thousand dollars of cash. You put some in your wallet, some in an envelope, and some in your shoes. If money is found in your wallet, that's where it's supposed to be. If it's found in an envelope, and it's all hundreds, and under $10,000, you should be able to convince law enforcement that you were on your way to purchase a rare rookie baseball card that you found on Craig's List. Alternatively, check Craig's List before you leave the cabin, and make sure you have something in mind. You might even call the seller and ask questions about the item. The money in your shoe is just in case you get robbed, then you'd have the ability to buy gas to get back to the cabin. Total, you should have less than $10,000 in the car.

You then want to go to a pawn shop, swap meet, or used computer retailer. You want to purchase a couple of desktop PC computers and a screwdriver. Get a monitor, keyboard, mouse, mouse pad, and everything needed to have a visibly working computer. Also pick up some duct tape and large plastic bags. The thing about desktop computers is that they common belief among the nontechnical is that the PC case is a magic box full of highly technical components. In reality, they are mostly hollow for air-flow purposes, minus the motherboard, hard drives, RAM, and PCI cards ,there isn't much in a PC case below the power supply. The other thing about desktop computers is that the police see them being transported all the time, and they aren't typically used for any illegal purpose. Assuming you look like Joe Businessman in a cheap suit, having a couple of computers in your car seems appropriate.

You could easily say that you and your spouse's computer contracted a virus, and you are on your way to the repair guy to have them fixed. Either way, a traffic stop is unlikely to warrant an inspection of the interior of a PC workstation. Police officers rarely carry tools for such a detailed inspection, and as they'd be liable for any damages, it's an expensive and unnecessary risk assuming you don't look like a drug dealer. If you drive a custom car with significant after-market modifications, then you do look like a drug dealer. In this case you'd want to buy a cheap car like a Honda Accord, Toyota Corolla, or etc. via Craig's List with cash under $10,000. Make as many trips back and forth to the cabins as necessary so that you never have more than $10,000 in the car at a time, minus what's hidden in the PC cases.

Generally speaking, the police need almost nothing to search a car in the US, but they generally need a warrant for a house, as long as no one is living there on parole or probation. Either of those give the police carte blanche to search any residence. If that's the case, you'd be better off renting a small office somewhere, but otherwise a home with your name on the mortgage and property tax records is better than any rental property. The goal here is to get the cash somewhere that is at least temporarily safe. Under no circumstances should you tell anyone anything, for any reason. Nor should you engage the assistance of others for any reason. If it wouldn't otherwise make you suspicious, you should turn your phone off as well. For this point in the example we will assume that you have got all the cash moved to your home safely with no one's help, via duct taping it in freezer backs into PC cases.

Now that you have your felonious cash at your home, you have a number of problems. No one will take a large amount of cash for anything without asking questions and filling out forms for the federal government. But as you are now on the verge of being truly wealthy, you have decided that you want to leave the poor weather of the US and move to the Caribbean. Buying a plane ticket with cash and then trying to board a plane with a lot of cash is a recipe for an encounter with Homeland Security at the airport. Don't do that. Do go out and buy prepaid Visa or MasterCard cards in $500 increments. Get ten of them. These are often available at the guest service desk of shopping malls; get gift cards, not prepaid debit cards. No Social Security Number is needed for gift cards. Learn where all the locations are that you can find for the purchase of these cards locally.

You will then get online and locate shelf companies for sale. The companies that are five years or older are credit worthy and thus are very expensive. Those that are under three years old are cheap. You will register your gift cards for online use using your own name, or whatever name your moral compass guides you to use. Then you will acquire ten of them. These are your companies now, new to you, but aged all the same. You will want to only choose from those located in your state, unless you live near a state border, in which case you could use a nearby state. Once you get all your corporate docs sent to you by email, you can contact the secretary of state to change the names on the corporations to your name. If you have a good ID for any other name, that works too, but again consult your moral compass. Once you have ten corporations under your control, you will want to put on your cheap suit, and go open corporate bank accounts for each corporation at completely different banks.

Before opening the bank accounts, or changing the address on the corporations, you may want to go rent ten offices, one for each company. Office leasing is pain-free, and usually has no ID requirements. Never use a virtual office or mail drop, as those addresses are listed in every bank's anti-fraud system for new accounts. Ideally, there would be ten bank accounts, in ten different corporate names, with ten different signer names, but it's perfectly legal for one man to work for ten companies. Maybe the man is an accountant, controller, or book keeper for a division of companies under a single corporate umbrella. It is necessary for whoever is opening the bank accounts to be listed as an officer for the corporation. Refer to the previous account opening section of this book again if necessary.

The goal is to obtain 10 fully functional bank accounts, with checks, deposit slips, and online account access. When setting up accounts, it would be a good idea to have a business card for each company, and it would be even better to have a website setup for each company as well. Using the prepaid gift cards, business cards can be purchased online, as can very cheap websites. It's important to pick industries for your new businesses that have some level of cash business. For example, convenience stores, auctions, salvage, lawn care, event management, or etc. would be businesses that have some level of cash business. A favorite is vending, any company that

170

has a number of vending machines, arcades, or change machines of any kind. Change machines don't usually accept 50 or 100 dollar bills, but the bank is only going to note cash versus check deposits, not the denominations.

Once the accounts are all setup, you will want to write checks from each account, to each account. For example, account #1 would get nine checks in random accounts under $5,000 each. The goal is to make deposits in such a way that you can add cash to each one, keeping the cash at below 30% of the deposit total. You may make 3 or 4 deposits per week for each account at first, and then after a few weeks move up to every weekday, with a 3x size deposit Monday morning, and another regular deposit on Monday afternoon or evening. Keep the deposits regular, and vary the signatures on the checks to match the signers. Work the volume and the amounts up over a six month period of time slow and steady. To increase the total input, you can add a credit card processor and use gift cards to pay your companies via credit cards. Within a few weeks you will be approaching the $100,000 mark in each account. Use the debit cards off the business accounts for any expenses that could possibly be attributed to a business. You can also buy cashier's checks, and money orders, with cash and deposit those as well. Stay under $3,000 on those.

You will want to open a bank account in the Bahamas or Cayman Islands via an Introduction Service. Choose a bank with other Caribbean branches. First Caribbean is a good choice. Once the account is setup there, you will make regular wires to the Bahamas in equal amounts each month, at the same time of the month. If asked, you are repaying a loan from a private equity company; loan documents can be found online. As the Bahamas and Cayman Islands are both fully compliant, you should have no problems sending out wires of $77,890 per month, or any other amount under $100K once per month, per company. Once you have the money in the Bahamas or Cayman, then it is time to go Antigua, Guatemala, Uruguay or St. Kitts to open a new account for a different offshore corporation. Ideally, you would open an account at each. Remember, smaller transactions less often attract less scrutiny than one large transaction. Once you have pushed the money into these other countries, it should be fairly safe.

Chapter 32: The Portable Millions Scenario

Wherever possible, you can add some privacy by utilizing the same banks. For example, if you transfer money from a First Caribbean account in the Bahamas to a First Caribbean Bank in Antigua, it would be booked as an internal transfer between banking clients. This is much more difficult for the US government to get a look at later especially as neither side of the transaction involved a US bank. Once the money is safely two steps removed from the US, you might consider Switzerland, Lichtenstein, Luxembourg, or Singapore for long term storage of the bulk of your wealth. You could easily setup access via a white card program as well. Never keep all your eggs in one basket. Stay diversified. It would also be a good idea to invest in new citizenships as well as soon as you can afford it. Anything you can do to distance yourself from a future IRS inquiry would be smart after successfully exiting the US with millions. Assuming your moral compass didn't guide you to send the IRS the 40% they think they deserve of course.

The Portable Millions Scenario

As an alternative to using corporate accounts, and traditional banking, there is an additional option for those that are technically adept. One could quite easily buy thousands of prepaid gift cards of the MasterCard/Visa variety by simply traveling around the country. The problem is the transportation of the cash, assuming that's done carefully, or if you elect to just work slowly buying up cards locally, that could work too. If you were to purchase a mag-strip reader/writer and dye sublimation printer with PVC card stock, you'd be all set. With the above, you have all you need to store the card data and reprint new cards. In this case you'd buy the card, copy it's data via the mag-reader to a hard drive or thumb drive, put the card's CVV2 numbers and expiration date in a spreadsheet next to the card number then shred the card.

The result is all of your money would be in a virtual state in a USB drive you can encrypt and carry in your pocket. Alternatively, you could compress the data, encrypt it, and up load the file to any online storage provider such as Carbonite. In this scenario you'd be able to travel with no debit cards, or anything else to link you to the fortune you have zipped up online. You could even mail your dye sublimation printer to yourself in whatever country you plan to relocate to. This may be an ideal scenario for anyone whose finances and banking are already under a lot of scrutiny. Or, if you have no access to new ID for banking, and choose not to use your own, this situation would work for you. You wouldn't want to travel with stacks of cards of course.

Once you arrive to a new country, you can use the card numbers to buy virtual currencies, or setup a credit card processing account, and "process" each card number. This could be done without printing a single card. If all else fails, you could fire up the dye sublimation printer (these are around $5,000 for one that does decent volume) and reprint the identical cards. Cards can be cashed in banks, Western Union, or used for actual purchases. These cards don't usually have a name on them, but there is nothing keeping you from adding one, giving the card the appearance of a prepaid debit card versus a gift card. This would allow the card to be used for car rentals, hotels, and a wider variety of in-person activities outside the United States.

A much slower system utilizing the same principles could be executed with a credit card processing account via Square, Intuit, or any major process. You would at least need a single business account, but many may be necessary for larger volumes of conversion of cash into actual money in a bank. Square and Intuit have portable devices that connect to smart phones and enable a small business to accept physical cards. Once an account is setup and active, you could drive around buying cards, and swiping them as you go.

It would be unusual for a processor to see back to back transactions in even amounts. However, if you as a merchant sold an item that was $460 and the sales tax where are you located at is 8.25%, then the processor would expect to see transactions of $497.95 repeatedly. As long as these come in at regular intervals in a card-present transaction, there would be no red flags on the transactions. That being said, there are an uncountable number of algorithms working behind the scenes to detect regular credit card fraud, so it will be necessary to make sure you don't even appear to be doing anything similar to good old fashioned carding.

Each credit card processing account will have a limit, and they typically want to link the card processing account to a human being via a Social Security Number (and of course a credit check) this would be the dreaded Personal Guarantee. This is the greatest threat to financial privacy, and the one that creates the most obligation and risk. This would be a bad idea in most circumstances, unless of course you were truly leaving the US permanently. If that was the case though, there are dozens of ways to "cash out" your whole life in the US in much more profitable ways.

Chapter 33: The Golden Parachute Scenario

There are a vast number of Americans poorly prepared for retirement. Men and women that have worked hard their whole life only to see their investments fail to produce adequate dividends when they need it most. Pension plans have failed, the cost of living has risen, and inflation has taken its toll. With the economy in the US and Europe in dire straits, many older citizens would certainly leave it all behind for a life on the beach somewhere. Compared to working 40 hour weeks for little pay well into your 80s, it is the logical conclusion to come to. The state of the economy is not your fault. The government's inability to manage a budget is not your fault. Why should you be punished for the mistakes of others simply because you share a nationality?

On the other hand, many Americans have not worked harp their whole life. Almost 50% of the US doesn't pay taxes, and lives off some form of government assistance. Others have bounced from bankruptcy to bankruptcy via sub-prime mortgages they shouldn't have been approved for to begin with. In both cases, these citizens here cost the tax payers billions of dollars, either directly with social programs, or indirectly via the bank bailouts. There is an obvious contrast here between those that are financially responsible, and those that aren't and yet both paths end in the same place; retiring into a near-poverty state in a bad economy. The difference is that those of you that worked your whole life never got your hand-outs. What if there was a way to go back and do it all again; would you ride the system this time? What if you could get a check today for all the money you have saved the government and corporate America in one lump sum; would you take it?

There is a way to do just that, without having to go back and live a life on government assistance. Hundreds of thousands of people personally bankrupt each year, and thousands of companies do the same. Statistically, one extra wouldn't be a needle in a haystack, it would be a needle in a haystack full of needles. If you created a business that paid you a huge salary and bonuses, that failed, does that make you a criminal? As half of Wall Street isn't in jail, the answer is no. The question should be what makes those guys special, and how is their hard work any more deserving of reward than yours is? The difference between them and you is likely only that they know how to game the system and you do not, but that is about to change.

Before going into the details, one must understand how successful businesses get started. Gone are the days where you could start a business in your garage and later sell it for millions. Successful businesses are funded by private equity companies. Even so, most businesses fail in the first three years. If you poured your life savings into a business, took out a second mortgage on the home, and wipe out your children's college fund, the failure of your business could lead you to personal bankruptcy. People in the business of business know better. Never personally guarantee anything, and never commingle personal credit and a business; those are amateur mistakes that banks prey upon. Your modern day CEO will begin a business from an aged shelf-corporation and fund the whole project with someone else's money, and rely on corporate credit not personal guarantees. Some CEOs have gone from company to company for years, creating multi-million dollar ventures, guaranteeing a $200K salary for themselves, and riding down the failure of one business after another.

The savviest even have figured out ways to profit from a failed business. And why should the CEO suffer personally for a failed business? Would anyone invest in a corporation if they could be personally bankrupted by the investment? Would you buy stock in Apple, or Google if you could suddenly become responsible for their debt if they fail? No, that's not how it works. We each make investments with the understanding that the maximum we could lose, is 100% of the investment, and no more. Why would you do any different with your own business? Either way, a troubled business is more work, not less, so shouldn't you at least get the same salary?

Regardless of your previous business experience, anyone can start a business. That fact probably has a lot to do with the fact that a very high percentage of businesses fail, but in this case that's a good thing. In the following hypothetical example, a business person would create a business out of a 5+ year old shelf corporation, massage the credit, and take on a full debt load within six months. As corporate credit works completely differently than personal credit, this is easily doable, and done every day. The trick is to take on small lines of credit, pay the bills, and to very quickly work your way up to larger credit lines. Building corporate credit is a rather detailed subject that would fill another book entirely. But the short of it is that you must get the lines of credit that you can, use them, and then pay the minimum balance plus 10% on time. Dun and Bradstreet (D&B) is the predominate business credit reporting agency. By monitoring your D&B report very carefully, you can apply for larger and larger credit lines.

It's very easy to get into a few million dollars of debt in six months. If your business can make the payments on that debt (even if it's from the sale of what you've financed) then you'd easily qualify for a multi-million dollar loan, especially if you had amassed enough cash to pay 10%-20% down on the loan. It isn't exactly good business to finance goods, machinery, computers, and then to sell them to pay the bills. This is basically giving yourself a cash loan. Obviously you could simply run up the bills and flee the country, leaving behind the debt. Or, you could pay yourself a huge salary, and bonuses, and then quit your job and walk away. The results are exactly the same, the only difference is paperwork.

This hypothetical example is likely frowned upon by banks, commercial lenders, and federal governments. Nevertheless, there is no law against owing money in the US or UK (if there were, more people would be in jail than out). There are so many failed businesses every single day that the government couldn't possibly review them all and score them based on who really tried hard, versus those that really only put in the hours for the salary and bonuses. Obviously there are no laws against being a bad business person either. Some of the most successful business owners and CEOs have had dozens of failed businesses, and in most cases, they have many more failed businesses than successful ones. If your company made bad offshore investments that didn't pan out, then that's just how it goes. A smart business person might even choose to finance a new offshore venture in this manner, allowing a US business to fail in order to prop up one in a better taxation environment. It's just good business, even if the US banks don't see it that way.

Chapter 34: The Full Commitment Scenario

In the previous section we discussed how to create your own Golden Parachute, and how to cash out the corporation for personal gain putting yourself first, instead of the corporation. Ethical or not, it's how it's done, and it's done every day. No CEO is going to willfully go down with the ship, that's just not a logical course of action. Ultimately all the debt will be covered out of the loss reserves from big banks that profit from predatory lending practices, and prey upon the unwary with a full arsenal of financial instruments designed to maximize their profits. Worst case scenario, the governments bail out the banks; that's how the system works. You can complain about it, lobby against it, and vote accordingly, and maybe with years of hard work (for which you don't be paid) you might be able to change big government. That's a big challenge. For many of us, the beach is a better option.

To get to the beach, you may need to liquidate a few assets. In the previous section we discussed paying yourself a large salary with bonuses, but you could easily liquidate the company and leave the country. That could be considered fraud, but if you were to continue to make small payments while patronizing your creditors, you'd simply blend in with all the other failed businesses. Just for fun, you can call the FBI and tell them that you have a client that you extended credit to, that later defaulted and hasn't paid you. They will tell you it's a civil issue for the civil courts. They won't touch anything under $120,000, and as the government approaches bankruptcy itself, they will have to raise the bar on what they do handle, not lower it. An account that is $120,000+ with no payments might get some action. A $60,000 debt where the client made six months worth of payments never will, that's just bad business. With that in mind, if your business had a large number of accounts, all under $60K, and you made a few payments, you could feasibly liquidate and walk away with millions, leaving no possibility of investigation behind.

Using a fake ID or committing any acts of intentional deceit, can be considered fraud. In certain circumstances it may be smart to utilize your real identity, to use your SSN, and maybe even sign a personal guarantee. In spite of all previous advice to the contrary, there is one scenario where it could be advantageous to fully commit to a deal personally. In the previous scenario we discussed maximizing corporate credit. It is also possible to maximize personal credit. The problem with personal credit is simple: opening new accounts lowers your credit score, so it's not easy to "cash-out". The credit reporting agencies Experian, Equifax, and TransUnion all penalize individuals for inquiries and new accounts. They do not penalize individual credit profiles for personal guarantees, as they have no idea how many you have signed or for what company.

Therefore, it is possible to build up a corporation from a shelf corporation, getting it to perfect credit levels, and then extending its capacity for debt with a personal guarantee. This is exactly what the banks want you to do. You could even take out a home equity loan, and put more down on a large corporate loan. All of this is a very bad idea unless you plan to ruin your credit, and lose your home. That is rarely a good idea, unless your plan is to take the millions of dollars from the corporate loans and leave the country. And by that we of course mean to invest in offshore ventures that require personal oversight and attention for years.

In this scenario someone could maximize their lifetime of good credit, and build their own retirement plan on a beach somewhere. This technique will not win you friends in domestic banks or governments. But again, there is no law against owing money, and who's to say how hard you tried to get those bills paid? After all, you sank everything you owned into the venture, and personally guaranteed the deals; exactly what the banks expect you to do. What's suspicious about that? Sure, if a US company invested millions in a partner company in Uruguay it's a risky venture from the US perspective. But it's a lot less risky if you own the Uruguayan company too via nominees.

Bank and Switch

The most common scenario for most people is not going to involve a duffel bag full of cash. In spite of the lack of financial privacy available, most people use conventional bank accounts, often linked to their personal name. It usually takes some kind of event to wake up a law abiding citizen to the fact that the governments and banks don't play fair. It's only then that they will feel compelled to buy a book like this, and make a change in their financial habits. Considering the obvious fiscal problems in the United States and Europe, these events are going to become more and more common. You can't expect all the people on welfare, disability, and unemployment to go out and get jobs tomorrow, that isn't going to happen. Thus, the big governments will continue to redistribute wealth robbing from the rich to give to the poor. And these days anyone working for a living that makes a reasonable income can be considered rich enough to rob. Taxes are going up, and there are more and more social programs every election cycle. Socialism is great, if you are on the receiving end, not if you are paying all the bills. As long as politicians can use social welfare (i.e. free money), to legally buy votes, this trend will continue, and so will the all-out assault on wealth. If you are reading this book, chances are you are looking for a way out.

The best way out is to simply leave the high-tax domicile. For many of you, that would mean leaving your home country. Sadly, most Americans think the United States is an island that you can't leave, or wouldn't want to since only America has Starbucks, Wal-Mart, McDonald's, and free Wi-Fi, right? Those of you reading this via free Wi-Fi at a McDonald's in Mexico will no doubt find this amusing. Nevertheless, the media supported "American Exceptional ism" has led many otherwise intelligent human beings to fear leaving their country in spite of the fact that it would be cheaper to have a much higher quality of life almost anywhere. For what it costs to live in the most expensive areas of the US, you could easily afford beach front property almost anywhere in the Caribbean. For those of you that can't bear the thought of leaving your families behind, that's understandable.

Of course there is always Skype to keep in touch with loved ones, and you could always send loved ones a plane ticket once a year for a Caribbean vacation at your house, but it's understandable either way. For those of you that wish to cash-out of the United States or other high-tax (and low privacy) nations, here's a hypothetical scenario that could be informative.

Let's assume you are a law abiding citizen with a 401K, savings account, a certificate of deposit (CD), and a few investments in the stock market. You have experienced low growth in all your investments, and high taxes in all your income, and you have decided to exit stage left. The goal is to get all of your assets liquidated and moved into the safety of offshore financial centers while keeping easy access to your wealth. In some cases many of you may want or need portable income to do this successfully. Although the employment opportunities for expatriates or Perpetual Travelers (PTs) is beyond the scope of this book, you will find a number of books on this subject available from any bookseller. One of the best books for someone just getting used to the idea of life outside their comfort zone is "Getting Out" by Mark Ehrman. This is an excellent book that covers life in various countries, including legal issues, quality of life, and other expectations.

Unfortunately, there are apparently no other guides for how one might liquefy his or her assets and safely leave a country like the US. It should be noted that the moment your investment profits are "fully realized" then they could become taxable. If you need to know how to best throw away 40%+ of your net worth, the IRS will be happy to advise you on where to send the check. If you wanted to skip that rather egregious part of the process, this is hypothetically how it could be done.

First things first, personal banking has severe limitations as to what is and is not suspicious. You will need a corporate bank account. Although aged shelf corporations always attract less attention than a newly filed corporation, for this scenario you could file a new corporation. Once you have a new corporation, it needs a commercial address (rent a cheap office), and then a bank account. The company could be a consulting firm, or any of a variety of different business models that would be international in nature. Pick a sold name such as: "NGO Systems", "TCP Technologies", or anything with a rather generic brand. Using acronyms usually opens up available options with the Secretary of State's database (where corporations are listed). In this case, you will also need an offshore account as well, and in the same name. You aren't trying to hide anything here, you are using your real ID, SSN, and passport. So create a corporation of the same name in your home state/country, and the Bahamas or Cayman Islands.

Liquidating assets can be tricky, but if it's done at the beginning of the year you would have a whole year to work with before tax time. In this scenario you are going to liquidate all your assets and pour them into your new business. What could be more common? Banks see this type of activity pretty regularly. As long as your name is all over the personal assets, and the corporation, the banks don't ask any questions. As long as the funds come into the corporate account from sources that can be documented, like your brokerage account, or your savings account, you'll be fine. In the case of CDs, if they are locked into a certain term, you can always take a loan against them. You could even add a private equity loan to pool more cash for your business. Let's assume for our hypothetical example that you have amassed $500, 000 into your business' account.

Your goal is to of course get all of the money out of the United States, permanently. At this point you have several options. Let's assume that your bank account in the Bahamas is with First Caribbean, and your money in the US is with Chase. You will go visit your Chase banker in person. You will ask about a business loan, and you will say you need $5 million to fund your company's expansion into certain projects. The point is not to get the loan, it's to let the banker know you are in the market for a loan. No matter what they offer, it's not good enough. Just telling them you plan to invest it in projects in Central America will cause them to push away from the table. Wait a few weeks and return, and tell the Chase banker that you think you have a deal with First Caribbean to fund your company's projects. Obviously they'd be a better match for this project. You might actually want to talk to First Caribbean about a loan, and have a representative there. Don't sign anything, don't do a deal, but do everything else you can to accumulate documentation that you are trying to get the loan.

When you return to Chase, you will tell them you believe you have secured the deal with First Caribbean, and that you will need to wire the 20% to cover your down payment on the loan, and that there will be a $5 million wire back to chase at some point later. Both of these wires will trigger an IRS form, and a Suspicious Transaction Form, however, as soon as the bank's security/compliance department calls your business banker he'll fill them in on your project as you have discussed it with him, they'd have no reason to hold the wire up . In fact, they wouldn't want to do anything to screw up the opportunity to help you "manage" the $5 million. The wire from Chase will not have any problems. Once the money is in the Bahamas, it's off the radar for the US. They can subpoena the records of the transactions later, but they'd no longer be able to control the transactions. At that point, you need to move the money into many other offshore corporate accounts in Antigua, Guatemala, and Uruguay. Document every transaction, as if they were made by your US company, as the IRS expects you to.

At the end of the year, you will need to file an 1120 Corporate Tax Return to the IRS for your company, and a personal tax return. Those filings should detail the fact that you sank all your personal money into a business, and your business paid out vendors, consultants, supplies, and etc. Thus you have a huge loss for the year, and neither you nor your company owe any taxes. The IRS would of course expect you to return a profit eventually, and pay taxes on it, but there is nothing keeping you from folding the company on January 1st, and dissolving it legally in the state.

Bad business is not illegal. People make bad investments all the time. Worst case scenario the IRS may schedule you for an audit if they haven't seen any of that money returned in two to three years. By that time you could quite easily have renounced your US citizenship and eliminate the burden of being legally bound to pay taxes. Either way, if you don't leave a forwarding address, what can they do?

This example takes into consideration that big deals take time, and governments move slow, and it also exploits some gray areas in international tax laws involving the US. If you own the companies that ultimately received the money, the IRS could suggest tax fraud. However, if those corporations are offshore entities held by bearer shares, then that's an obstacle they can't overcome. Either way, who's to say those companies didn't pay out local vendors. Those financial wouldn't be exposed to the IRS anyway. For all the world, the paper trail for this scenario would look like you got suckered by some slick offshore business. Let them think it.

Conclusion

In the past few hypothetical examples we have examined various techniques that could be utilized by anyone willing to make the transition from a mediocre existence to the life of a wealthy expatriate. The trade-off could be personal debt, corporate debt, or tax obligations left behind. This is a course of action that should not be taken lightly. As the large governments teeter upon the pinnacles of their failed economic policy, they will be watching for those abandoning the sinking ship. Fortunately, with big government comes inefficiencies, loop holes, and large crevices in the laws often left behind by policy indirectly established by the lobbyists of large corporations. You don't have to be a multi-million dollar CEO to benefit from techniques they use; those tools are open for all.

The gray areas of the law can be treacherous, and there will always be a great rift between what's illegal versus what laws are actually enforced. You must do the research and plot your course carefully. Alternatively, although it may be illegal in most jurisdictions, a simple fake ID could eliminate 99% of the risk associated with creative banking and tax avoidance. If this would be a misdemeanor in your area, and your life depends on your successful relocation, then that risk/reward ratio should be very clear. Obviously the US doesn't post people's faces on wanted posters (and websites) for misdemeanors. At the other end of the spectrum, if you were to use someone else's identity, destroying their credit, or livelihood, then that's most likely a felony. There is never an excuse to destroy someone else's life to better your own, and so that should also be a very obvious choice you wouldn't want to make. That being said, this book is dedicated to the free exchange of information. Information that we hope can be used to give people back their freedom, their privacy, and in many cases their money as well.

The very thought that being born in any particular sovereign geography makes you obligated to pay that government 40%+ of all the money you make in life until death is absurd. You have a right to travel, a right to see the world, and a right to live wherever you choose to. Some of the worst economies exist in countries that expend the most effort to convince their citizens that they are the best place on Earth. That is insane. Somewhere in Detroit there is an unemployed man that is living in a home scheduled for foreclosure.

He lives off government assistance, and is barely surviving, and yet he most likely is still infected with American Exceptionalism; a patriot to the very end. Countries need people like that to die on the front lines of foreign wars for their fleeting political ambitions. If that's your course in life, more power to you, we hope your next of kin gets a shiny medal to remember you by.

For those of you that are a little more selfish, greedy, or in most cases intelligent, you will find a much higher quality of life in the Caribbean. For the maximum amount of money one can get in welfare, food stamps, and assorted government assistance per month in the US you can live quite well in many other parts of the world. Of course you generally don't get "paid to stay" in the better countries to live in, so you will need some income; plan accordingly. The point is that it's a big world, and no one should be able to tell you what to do with your hard earned money. If a government wants 40%+ of your money then it's right to expect to see some return on investment, and not decades of mismanagement, politically motivated social programs, and wasted defense dollars. The patriots are fond of saying "if you don't like it, leave" and in this instance they are certainly right. Tens of thousands of people leave the US every year.

In 2012 the US actually had negative immigration from Mexico. That's to say that more people left the US and went to Mexico, than even came to the US from the poor border towns ravaged by the drug war. Mexico has a growing economy, with less than half the unemployment rate of the US. Meanwhile, politicians in the US are still trying to borrow billions from China to build a border wall. At least they will stop the drug traffic, right? I mean the drug cartels don't read maps, so they'd never notice the thousands of miles of unprotected US coastlines, right? In reality, the drug cartels own submarines, aircraft, and typically bribe their way through all ports of entry anyway. Nothing is going to change that. Meanwhile the US will continue to use The War on Drugs, The War on Terror, or The War on whatever is next to reduce civil liberties, and to target the financial privacy of anyone with any significant wealth. It's the way governments work. It can't be fixed.

On a less cynical note, the world financial systems are more porous than US borders. You don't have to suffer the indignity of being robbed repeatedly by a government. There is immense freedom of banking now, driven by emerging markets, and creative business models outside the traditional models. Today, a company called First Financial does mortgages for homeowners with no credit history, no pay-stubs, and no collateral. They send out human beings to evaluate the small businesses like street vendors, they talk to their peers, and they make a well advised credit decision. They are profitable, with only a 2% default rate, a tiny percentage of the US number. All over Africa people bank by cell phone and can make payments with their phone for goods and services. The world is evolving. There is great financial growth in many areas, and the opportunities that come with that growth.

If you choose to lock yourself into a single economy, that is your choice. With that choice you will be forced to ride the waves of economic despair associated with the financial systems allowed by your government. If you choose to broaden your horizons, and move your money to the international stage, then we hope the tools we have given you via this book will help you do that.

Suggested Reading

- "Future Crimes: Everything is connected, everyone is vulnerable, and what we can do about it" by Marc Goodman

- "No Place to Hide: Edward Snowden and the U.S. Surveillance State" by Glenn Greenwald

- "Mastering Bitcoin: Unlocking Digital Cryptocurrencies" by Andreas M. Antonopoulos

- "Automate This: How Algorithms took over our Markets, our Jobs, and the World" by Christopher Steiner

- "The Golden Ticket: P, NP and the Search for the Impossible" by Lance Fortnow

- "Dice World: Science and Life in a Random Universe" by Brian Clegg

- "Big Data" by Viktor Maye Schonberger and Kenneth Cukier

- "Industries of the Future" by Alec Ross

- "The Hacked World Order: How Nations Fight, Trade, Maneuver, and Manipulate in the Digital Age" by Adam Segal

- "Black Code: Surveillance, Privacy, and the Dark Side of the Internet" by Ronald J. Delbert

- "Glass Houses: Privacy, Secrecy, and Cyber Insecurity in a Transparent World" by Joel Brenner

- "The Dark Net: Inside the Digital Underground" by Jamie Bartlett

- "The Black Box Society: The Secret Algorithms that Control Money and Information" by Frank Pasquale

- "The Naked Future: What Happens in a World that Anticipates your Every Move" by Patrick Tucker

- "Discreet Mathematics with Applications" by Susanna S. Epp

Index

For more information on the subjects covered in The Covert Core Series, please visit the author's blog at:

https://www.cygonx.com

www.ingramcontent.com/pod-product-compliance
Lightning Source LLC
LaVergne TN
LVHW022343060326
832902LV00022B/4215